50 Meaty Restaurant Recipes for Home

By: Kelly Johnson

Table of Contents

- Beef Wellington
- Coq au Vin
- Braised Short Ribs
- Chicken Marsala
- Beef Stroganoff
- Prime Rib Roast
- Osso Buco
- Barbecue Brisket
- Balsamic Glazed Pork Tenderloin
- Lamb Chops with Rosemary
- Chicken Cacciatore
- Beef Bourguignon
- BBQ Ribs
- Roast Leg of Lamb
- Spaghetti Bolognese
- Pork Schnitzel
- Moroccan Lamb Tagine
- Veal Parmesan
- Beef Empanadas
- Duck Confit
- Meatloaf
- Beef Tacos
- Chicken Fried Steak
- Pork Belly Buns
- Beef and Ale Pie
- Chicken Alfredo
- Grilled Ribeye Steak
- Shrimp and Grits
- Stuffed Pork Chops
- Beef Fajitas
- Roast Beef and Yorkshire Pudding
- Chicken Satay

- Beef and Broccoli Stir-Fry
- Lamb Shank Braised in Red Wine
- Veal Scaloppini
- Pork Carnitas
- Stuffed Cabbage Rolls
- Chicken Kiev
- Beef Empanadas
- BBQ Chicken
- Slow Cooker Beef Chili
- Grilled Lamb Kebabs
- Shepherd's Pie
- Teriyaki Beef Skewers
- Peking Duck
- Beef Tenderloin with Horseradish Sauce
- Chicken and Sausage Gumbo
- Beef and Mushroom Pie
- Chicken Piccata
- Spicy Pork Ribs

Beef Wellington

Ingredients

For the Beef:

- 1.5 lb (700 g) beef tenderloin
- Salt and freshly ground black pepper
- 2 tbsp olive oil
- 2 tbsp Dijon mustard

For the Duxelles:

- 1 lb (450 g) mushrooms, finely chopped
- 2 tbsp unsalted butter
- 1 small shallot, minced
- 2 cloves garlic, minced
- 1/4 cup dry white wine
- 1 tsp fresh thyme leaves
- Salt and pepper to taste

For Assembly:

- 8 slices of prosciutto
- 1 sheet of puff pastry, thawed
- 1 egg, beaten (for egg wash)

Instructions

1. **Prepare the Beef:**
    - Season the beef tenderloin generously with salt and pepper.
    - Heat olive oil in a skillet over high heat. Sear the beef on all sides until browned (about 2 minutes per side). Remove from heat and let cool. Brush with Dijon mustard.
2. **Make the Duxelles:**
    - In a skillet, melt butter over medium heat. Add shallots and garlic, cooking until softened.
    - Add mushrooms and cook until they release their moisture and become golden brown, stirring occasionally.
    - Add wine and thyme, cook until the liquid evaporates. Season with salt and pepper. Let cool.
3. **Assemble the Wellington:**
    - Lay out the prosciutto slices on a piece of plastic wrap, slightly overlapping them.

        - Spread the cooled duxelles over the prosciutto.
        - Place the beef on top of the duxelles. Roll it up tightly in the prosciutto using the plastic wrap. Chill in the refrigerator for 15 minutes.
        - Roll out the puff pastry on a floured surface. Remove the beef from the plastic wrap and place it in the center of the pastry.
        - Fold the pastry over the beef and seal the edges. Brush with beaten egg.
4. **Bake:**
        - Preheat the oven to 400°F (200°C).
        - Place the wrapped beef on a baking sheet and brush with more beaten egg.
        - Bake for 25-30 minutes or until the pastry is golden brown and the internal temperature of the beef reaches 125°F (52°C) for medium-rare. Let rest for 10 minutes before slicing.

Enjoy your Beef Wellington!

Coq au Vin

Ingredients

- 1 whole chicken (about 4 lbs), cut into pieces
- Salt and freshly ground black pepper
- 2 tbsp vegetable oil
- 4 oz (115 g) pancetta or bacon, diced
- 1 large onion, chopped
- 2 carrots, sliced
- 3 cloves garlic, minced
- 2 tbsp all-purpose flour
- 2 cups red wine (such as Burgundy or Pinot Noir)
- 1 cup chicken broth
- 2 tbsp tomato paste
- 1 bouquet garni (a bundle of thyme, bay leaf, and parsley tied together)
- 8 oz (225 g) mushrooms, sliced
- 12 small pearl onions, peeled (or 1 large onion, chopped)
- 2 tbsp unsalted butter
- 1 tbsp chopped fresh parsley (for garnish)

Instructions

1. **Prepare the Chicken:**
    - Season the chicken pieces with salt and pepper.
2. **Brown the Chicken:**
    - Heat vegetable oil in a large Dutch oven or heavy pot over medium-high heat. Add the chicken pieces in batches, browning them on all sides. Remove and set aside.
3. **Cook the Pancetta:**
    - In the same pot, add the diced pancetta or bacon. Cook until crispy. Remove with a slotted spoon and set aside with the chicken.
4. **Sauté Vegetables:**
    - Add onions and carrots to the pot. Cook until softened, about 5 minutes. Add garlic and cook for an additional minute.
5. **Add Flour:**
    - Stir in the flour and cook for 2 minutes to create a roux.
6. **Deglaze and Simmer:**
    - Pour in the red wine, scraping up any browned bits from the bottom of the pot. Stir in the chicken broth and tomato paste. Add the bouquet garni.
7. **Combine Ingredients:**

- Return the chicken and pancetta to the pot. Bring to a simmer. Cover and cook on low heat for 45 minutes, or until the chicken is tender.

8. **Cook Mushrooms and Pearl Onions:**
    - While the chicken is cooking, melt butter in a skillet over medium heat. Add mushrooms and pearl onions. Sauté until golden brown, about 10 minutes. Set aside.
9. **Add Mushrooms and Onions:**
    - After 45 minutes, add the mushrooms and pearl onions to the pot with the chicken. Continue to cook, uncovered, for an additional 15 minutes.
10. **Final Touches:**
    - Remove the bouquet garni. Adjust seasoning with salt and pepper.
11. **Serve:**
    - Garnish with chopped parsley and serve with crusty bread or over mashed potatoes.

Enjoy your Coq au Vin!

Braised Short Ribs

Ingredients

4 lbs (1.8 kg) beef short ribs

Salt and freshly ground black pepper

2 tbsp vegetable oil

1 large onion, chopped

2 carrots, chopped

2 celery stalks, chopped

4 cloves garlic, minced

2 tbsp tomato paste

2 cups red wine (such as Cabernet Sauvignon or Merlot)

2 cups beef broth

1 cup water

2 tbsp Worcestershire sauce

2 sprigs fresh thyme

2 bay leaves

1 tbsp cornstarch (optional, for thickening)

2 tbsp water (optional, for cornstarch slurry)

Instructions

Prepare the Ribs:

Preheat the oven to 325°F (163°C).

Season the short ribs generously with salt and pepper.

Brown the Ribs:

Heat vegetable oil in a large Dutch oven or heavy oven-safe pot over medium-high heat. Add the short ribs in batches and brown on all sides, about 4-5 minutes per side. Remove and set aside.

Sauté Vegetables:

In the same pot, add onions, carrots, and celery. Cook until softened, about 5-7 minutes. Add garlic and cook for another minute.

Add Tomato Paste:

Stir in the tomato paste and cook for 2 minutes to caramelize.

Deglaze and Simmer:

Pour in the red wine, scraping up any browned bits from the bottom of the pot. Bring to a boil and cook for 2-3 minutes to reduce slightly.

Add beef broth, water, Worcestershire sauce, thyme, and bay leaves. Stir to combine.

Return Ribs and Braise:

Return the browned short ribs to the pot. The liquid should cover about 2/3 of the ribs. Bring to a simmer.

Transfer to Oven:

Cover the pot with a lid and transfer it to the preheated oven. Braise for 2.5 to 3 hours, or until the meat is tender and easily pulls away from the bone.

Finish the Sauce (Optional):

Remove the pot from the oven and transfer the ribs to a plate. Discard the thyme and bay leaves.

Skim off any excess fat from the surface of the sauce. For a thicker sauce, mix cornstarch with water to make a slurry and stir into the sauce. Simmer until thickened.

Serve:

Return the ribs to the pot, warm them through, and serve with mashed potatoes, polenta, or over noodles.

Enjoy your Braised Short Ribs!

Chicken Marsala

Ingredients

- 4 boneless, skinless chicken breasts
- Salt and freshly ground black pepper
- 1/2 cup all-purpose flour
- 4 tbsp unsalted butter, divided
- 2 tbsp olive oil
- 1 cup sliced mushrooms (cremini or button)
- 3/4 cup Marsala wine
- 1/2 cup chicken broth
- 1 tbsp chopped fresh parsley (for garnish)

Instructions

1. **Prepare the Chicken:**
   - Place the chicken breasts between two sheets of plastic wrap or parchment paper. Pound them to an even thickness, about 1/2 inch, using a meat mallet or rolling pin.
   - Season both sides of the chicken with salt and pepper. Dredge each piece in flour, shaking off the excess.
2. **Cook the Chicken:**
   - In a large skillet, heat 2 tbsp of butter and 2 tbsp of olive oil over medium-high heat.
   - Add the chicken breasts and cook until golden brown on both sides, about 4-5 minutes per side. Remove the chicken from the skillet and set aside.
3. **Sauté the Mushrooms:**
   - In the same skillet, add the remaining 2 tbsp of butter. Add the sliced mushrooms and cook until they are browned and tender, about 5 minutes.
4. **Make the Sauce:**
   - Pour in the Marsala wine, scraping up any browned bits from the bottom of the pan. Bring to a boil and cook for 2-3 minutes to reduce slightly.
   - Add the chicken broth and continue to simmer for another 3 minutes.
5. **Combine and Simmer:**
   - Return the chicken to the skillet, spooning some of the sauce and mushrooms over the top. Simmer for about 5-7 minutes, or until the chicken is cooked through and the sauce has thickened.
6. **Finish and Serve:**
   - Garnish with chopped fresh parsley.
   - Serve hot with sides like pasta, mashed potatoes, or a fresh vegetable.

Enjoy your Chicken Marsala!

Beef Stroganoff

Ingredients

- 1.5 lbs (700 g) beef sirloin or tenderloin, thinly sliced into strips
- Salt and freshly ground black pepper
- 2 tbsp vegetable oil
- 1 medium onion, finely chopped
- 2 cloves garlic, minced
- 8 oz (225 g) mushrooms, sliced
- 2 tbsp all-purpose flour
- 1 cup beef broth
- 1 cup sour cream
- 2 tbsp Dijon mustard
- 1 tbsp Worcestershire sauce
- 2 tbsp chopped fresh parsley (for garnish)
- Cooked egg noodles, rice, or mashed potatoes (for serving)

Instructions

1. **Prepare the Beef:**
    - Season the beef strips with salt and pepper.
2. **Brown the Beef:**
    - Heat vegetable oil in a large skillet or sauté pan over medium-high heat.
    - Add the beef in batches and cook until browned on all sides, about 2-3 minutes per batch. Remove beef and set aside.
3. **Sauté Vegetables:**
    - In the same skillet, add a little more oil if needed and cook the onion until translucent, about 3-4 minutes.
    - Add garlic and mushrooms, and cook until mushrooms are browned and tender, about 5 minutes.
4. **Make the Sauce:**
    - Stir in the flour and cook for 1-2 minutes to remove the raw flour taste.
    - Gradually add the beef broth while stirring, and bring to a simmer. Cook for 2-3 minutes, or until the sauce starts to thicken.
5. **Combine and Simmer:**
    - Reduce heat to low and stir in the sour cream, Dijon mustard, and Worcestershire sauce.
    - Return the beef to the skillet and cook gently for another 5 minutes, or until the beef is heated through and the sauce is well combined.
6. **Serve:**
    - Garnish with chopped parsley.

- Serve over cooked egg noodles, rice, or mashed potatoes.

Enjoy your Beef Stroganoff!

Prime Rib Roast

Ingredients

- 1 (5-7 lbs) bone-in prime rib roast
- Salt and freshly ground black pepper
- 2 tbsp olive oil
- 4 cloves garlic, minced
- 2 tbsp fresh rosemary, chopped (or 2 tsp dried)
- 2 tbsp fresh thyme, chopped (or 2 tsp dried)
- 1 tbsp Dijon mustard
- 1 cup beef broth
- 1 cup red wine (optional)
- 2 tbsp all-purpose flour (optional, for gravy)

Instructions

1. **Prepare the Roast:**
    - Preheat your oven to 450°F (230°C).
    - Pat the prime rib roast dry with paper towels. Season generously with salt and pepper.
2. **Make the Herb Paste:**
    - In a small bowl, combine olive oil, garlic, rosemary, thyme, and Dijon mustard to form a paste.
3. **Apply the Herb Paste:**
    - Rub the herb paste all over the roast, ensuring it's well coated.
4. **Roast the Meat:**
    - Place the roast bone-side down on a rack in a roasting pan.
    - Roast in the preheated oven for 15 minutes to develop a crust.
    - Reduce the oven temperature to 325°F (165°C) and continue to roast for about 1.5 to 2.5 hours, or until the internal temperature reaches your desired doneness:
        - **Rare:** 120°F (49°C)
        - **Medium Rare:** 130°F (54°C)
        - **Medium:** 140°F (60°C)
        - **Medium Well:** 150°F (66°C)
        - **Well Done:** 160°F (71°C)
    - Use a meat thermometer to check the temperature.
5. **Rest the Meat:**
    - Remove the roast from the oven and let it rest for at least 15-20 minutes before carving. This helps the juices redistribute.
6. **Make the Gravy (Optional):**
    - If you'd like gravy, place the roasting pan on the stove over medium heat.

- Add the beef broth and red wine to the pan, scraping up any browned bits from the bottom.
- Bring to a simmer and cook until reduced slightly, about 5 minutes.
- For a thicker gravy, mix 2 tbsp flour with a little water to make a slurry, and stir into the simmering liquid. Cook until thickened.

7. **Serve:**
   - Slice the roast and serve with the gravy, if desired.

Enjoy your Prime Rib Roast!

Osso Buco

Ingredients

- 4 (1.5-2 inch thick) veal shanks (osso buco)
- Salt and freshly ground black pepper
- 1/4 cup all-purpose flour
- 2 tbsp olive oil
- 2 tbsp unsalted butter
- 1 large onion, chopped
- 2 carrots, chopped
- 2 celery stalks, chopped
- 4 cloves garlic, minced
- 1 cup dry white wine
- 1 cup chicken broth
- 1 can (14.5 oz) crushed tomatoes
- 2 tbsp tomato paste
- 1 tbsp fresh thyme leaves (or 1 tsp dried)
- 2 bay leaves
- 1/2 cup chopped fresh parsley (for gremolata)
- 2 tbsp lemon zest (for gremolata)
- 2 cloves garlic, minced (for gremolata)

Instructions

1. **Prepare the Shanks:**
    - Season veal shanks generously with salt and pepper. Dredge each shank in flour, shaking off the excess.
2. **Brown the Shanks:**
    - Heat olive oil and butter in a large Dutch oven or heavy pot over medium-high heat.
    - Add the veal shanks and brown on all sides, about 4-5 minutes per side. Remove shanks and set aside.
3. **Sauté Vegetables:**
    - In the same pot, add onion, carrots, and celery. Cook until vegetables are softened, about 5-7 minutes.
    - Add garlic and cook for an additional minute.
4. **Deglaze the Pot:**
    - Pour in the white wine, scraping up any browned bits from the bottom of the pot. Bring to a boil and cook for 2-3 minutes to reduce slightly.
5. **Add Liquids and Seasonings:**

- Stir in chicken broth, crushed tomatoes, tomato paste, thyme, and bay leaves. Mix well.

6. **Combine and Braise:**
   - Return the veal shanks to the pot. The liquid should come about halfway up the sides of the shanks.
   - Bring to a simmer. Cover and cook in the preheated oven at 325°F (165°C) for about 2.5 to 3 hours, or until the meat is tender and falling off the bone.

7. **Prepare Gremolata:**
   - While the osso buco is cooking, mix together chopped parsley, lemon zest, and minced garlic in a small bowl.

8. **Finish and Serve:**
   - Remove the pot from the oven and discard the bay leaves. Adjust seasoning with salt and pepper if needed.
   - Serve the osso buco with the gremolata sprinkled on top. It pairs well with risotto, polenta, or crusty bread.

Enjoy your Osso Buco!

Barbecue Brisket

Ingredients

- 5-6 lbs (2.3-2.7 kg) beef brisket
- 2 tbsp olive oil
- Salt and freshly ground black pepper
- 2 tbsp paprika
- 1 tbsp brown sugar
- 1 tbsp garlic powder
- 1 tbsp onion powder
- 1 tbsp ground cumin
- 1 tsp cayenne pepper (optional, for heat)
- 1 cup beef broth
- 1 cup barbecue sauce (your favorite brand or homemade)

Instructions

1. **Prepare the Brisket:**
   - Preheat your oven to 300°F (150°C).
   - Trim excess fat from the brisket, leaving a thin layer for flavor.
2. **Season the Brisket:**
   - In a small bowl, mix together paprika, brown sugar, garlic powder, onion powder, cumin, cayenne pepper (if using), salt, and pepper.
   - Rub the spice mixture evenly over all sides of the brisket.
3. **Sear the Brisket:**
   - Heat olive oil in a large skillet over medium-high heat. Sear the brisket on all sides until browned, about 4-5 minutes per side.
4. **Prepare for Braising:**
   - Transfer the seared brisket to a roasting pan or a large Dutch oven.
   - Pour beef broth around the brisket (not over it to keep the seasoning intact).
5. **Cook the Brisket:**
   - Cover the pan tightly with aluminum foil or a lid.
   - Roast in the preheated oven for about 4-5 hours, or until the brisket is tender and can be easily shredded with a fork.
6. **Apply Barbecue Sauce:**
   - Remove the brisket from the oven and discard the foil or lid.
   - Brush barbecue sauce over the brisket.
   - Return the brisket to the oven, uncovered, and bake for an additional 30 minutes, or until the sauce is caramelized.
7. **Rest and Slice:**

        - Remove the brisket from the oven and let it rest for at least 15 minutes before slicing.
        - Slice against the grain for the best texture.
8. **Serve:**
        - Serve the brisket with extra barbecue sauce on the side. It pairs well with coleslaw, baked beans, or cornbread.

Enjoy your Barbecue Brisket!

Balsamic Glazed Pork Tenderloin

Ingredients

- 5-6 lbs (2.3-2.7 kg) beef brisket
- 2 tbsp olive oil
- Salt and freshly ground black pepper
- 2 tbsp paprika
- 1 tbsp brown sugar
- 1 tbsp garlic powder
- 1 tbsp onion powder
- 1 tbsp ground cumin
- 1 tsp cayenne pepper (optional, for heat)
- 1 cup beef broth
- 1 cup barbecue sauce (your favorite brand or homemade)

Instructions

1. **Prepare the Brisket:**
    - Preheat your oven to 300°F (150°C).
    - Trim excess fat from the brisket, leaving a thin layer for flavor.
2. **Season the Brisket:**
    - In a small bowl, mix together paprika, brown sugar, garlic powder, onion powder, cumin, cayenne pepper (if using), salt, and pepper.
    - Rub the spice mixture evenly over all sides of the brisket.
3. **Sear the Brisket:**
    - Heat olive oil in a large skillet over medium-high heat. Sear the brisket on all sides until browned, about 4-5 minutes per side.
4. **Prepare for Braising:**
    - Transfer the seared brisket to a roasting pan or a large Dutch oven.
    - Pour beef broth around the brisket (not over it to keep the seasoning intact).
5. **Cook the Brisket:**
    - Cover the pan tightly with aluminum foil or a lid.
    - Roast in the preheated oven for about 4-5 hours, or until the brisket is tender and can be easily shredded with a fork.
6. **Apply Barbecue Sauce:**
    - Remove the brisket from the oven and discard the foil or lid.
    - Brush barbecue sauce over the brisket.
    - Return the brisket to the oven, uncovered, and bake for an additional 30 minutes, or until the sauce is caramelized.
7. **Rest and Slice:**

- Remove the brisket from the oven and let it rest for at least 15 minutes before slicing.
    - Slice against the grain for the best texture.
8. **Serve:**
    - Serve the brisket with extra barbecue sauce on the side. It pairs well with coleslaw, baked beans, or cornbread.

Enjoy your Barbecue Brisket!

Balsamic Glazed Pork Tenderloin

Ingredients

- 1.5 lbs (680 g) pork tenderloin
- Salt and freshly ground black pepper
- 2 tbsp olive oil
- 1/2 cup balsamic vinegar
- 1/4 cup honey
- 2 tbsp Dijon mustard
- 2 cloves garlic, minced
- 1 tbsp fresh rosemary, chopped (or 1 tsp dried)
- 1 tbsp fresh thyme, chopped (or 1 tsp dried)
- 1/2 cup chicken broth
- 1 tbsp cornstarch (optional, for thickening)
- 1 tbsp water (optional, for cornstarch slurry)

Instructions

1. **Prepare the Pork:**
   - Preheat your oven to 400°F (200°C).
   - Season the pork tenderloin generously with salt and pepper.
2. **Sear the Pork:**
   - Heat olive oil in an oven-safe skillet over medium-high heat.
   - Add the pork tenderloin and sear on all sides until browned, about 2-3 minutes per side. Remove from the skillet and set aside.
3. **Make the Balsamic Glaze:**
   - In the same skillet, add balsamic vinegar, honey, Dijon mustard, minced garlic, rosemary, and thyme.
   - Bring to a simmer, stirring frequently, until the mixture reduces by half, about 5-7 minutes. The glaze should be thickened and syrupy.
4. **Combine and Roast:**
   - Return the seared pork tenderloin to the skillet, turning to coat it in the glaze.
   - Transfer the skillet to the preheated oven.
   - Roast for 20-25 minutes, or until the internal temperature of the pork reaches 145°F (63°C).
5. **Make the Sauce (Optional):**
   - If you want a thicker sauce, remove the pork from the skillet and set aside to rest.
   - Stir 1 tbsp cornstarch into 1 tbsp water to make a slurry. Add to the remaining glaze in the skillet and simmer for a few minutes until thickened.
6. **Rest and Slice:**
   - Let the pork rest for 5-10 minutes before slicing.

7. **Serve:**
    - Serve the sliced pork tenderloin with extra balsamic glaze drizzled on top. It pairs well with roasted vegetables, mashed potatoes, or a fresh salad.

Enjoy your Balsamic Glazed Pork Tenderloin!

Lamb Chops with Rosemary

Ingredients

- 8 lamb chops (about 1-inch thick)
- Salt and freshly ground black pepper
- 2 tbsp olive oil
- 3 cloves garlic, minced
- 2 tbsp fresh rosemary, chopped (or 2 tsp dried rosemary)
- 1 tbsp fresh lemon juice (optional)
- 1 tbsp Dijon mustard (optional)

Instructions

1. **Prepare the Lamb Chops:**
   - Pat the lamb chops dry with paper towels. Season both sides generously with salt and pepper.
2. **Make the Marinade:**
   - In a small bowl, mix together olive oil, minced garlic, chopped rosemary, lemon juice, and Dijon mustard (if using).
3. **Marinate the Lamb Chops:**
   - Rub the marinade evenly over both sides of the lamb chops. For best results, marinate for at least 30 minutes at room temperature or up to 2 hours in the refrigerator. If marinating in the fridge, let the lamb come to room temperature before cooking.
4. **Cook the Lamb Chops:**
   Grilling Method:
   - Preheat your grill to medium-high heat.
   - Grill the lamb chops for about 3-4 minutes per side for medium-rare, or until they reach your desired level of doneness. Use a meat thermometer to check: 125°F (52°C) for medium-rare, 135°F (57°C) for medium, and 145°F (63°C) for medium-well.
5. **Pan-Seared Method:**
   - Heat a large skillet over medium-high heat. Add a little olive oil if needed.
   - Sear the lamb chops for about 3-4 minutes per side for medium-rare, or until they reach your desired level of doneness. Use a meat thermometer to check.
6. **Rest the Lamb Chops:**
   - Remove the lamb chops from the heat and let them rest for 5 minutes before serving. This allows the juices to redistribute and keeps the meat tender.
7. **Serve:**
   - Serve the lamb chops hot, garnished with extra rosemary if desired. They pair well with roasted vegetables, a fresh salad, or mashed potatoes.

Enjoy your Lamb Chops with Rosemary!

Chicken Cacciatore

Ingredients

- 4 bone-in, skinless chicken thighs
- 4 bone-in, skinless chicken drumsticks
- Salt and freshly ground black pepper
- 2 tbsp olive oil
- 1 large onion, chopped
- 2 cloves garlic, minced
- 1 red bell pepper, chopped
- 1 green bell pepper, chopped
- 1 cup mushrooms, sliced
- 1 cup dry white wine (optional)
- 1 can (14.5 oz) diced tomatoes
- 1/2 cup tomato paste
- 1 cup chicken broth
- 1 tsp dried oregano
- 1 tsp dried basil
- 1/2 tsp red pepper flakes (optional)
- 1/2 cup black olives, sliced (optional)
- 2 tbsp capers (optional)
- 2 tbsp fresh parsley, chopped (for garnish)
- Cooked pasta, rice, or crusty bread (for serving)

Instructions

1. **Prepare the Chicken:**
    - Season the chicken thighs and drumsticks with salt and pepper.
2. **Brown the Chicken:**
    - Heat olive oil in a large skillet or Dutch oven over medium-high heat.
    - Add the chicken pieces and brown on all sides, about 5-7 minutes. Remove chicken and set aside.
3. **Sauté Vegetables:**
    - In the same skillet, add the onion, garlic, red bell pepper, green bell pepper, and mushrooms. Cook until vegetables are softened, about 5 minutes.
4. **Deglaze the Pan:**
    - Pour in the white wine (if using) and cook for 2-3 minutes, scraping up any browned bits from the bottom of the pan.
5. **Add Tomatoes and Seasonings:**
    - Stir in the diced tomatoes, tomato paste, chicken broth, oregano, basil, and red pepper flakes (if using). Mix well.

6. **Combine and Simmer:**
    - Return the browned chicken to the skillet, along with any juices that have accumulated. The liquid should come about halfway up the sides of the chicken.
    - Bring to a simmer. Cover and cook for 30-40 minutes, or until the chicken is cooked through and tender.
7. **Add Olives and Capers (Optional):**
    - If using, stir in the black olives and capers during the last 10 minutes of cooking.
8. **Finish and Serve:**
    - Garnish with chopped fresh parsley.
    - Serve hot over cooked pasta, rice, or with crusty bread.

Enjoy your Chicken Cacciatore!

Beef Bourguignon

Ingredients

- 3 lbs (1.4 kg) beef chuck, cut into 1.5-inch cubes
- Salt and freshly ground black pepper
- 3 tbsp vegetable oil
- 6 oz (170 g) bacon or pancetta, diced
- 1 large onion, chopped
- 2 carrots, sliced
- 3 cloves garlic, minced
- 2 tbsp all-purpose flour
- 2 cups red wine (such as Burgundy or Pinot Noir)
- 2 cups beef broth
- 1 tbsp tomato paste
- 1 bouquet garni (a bundle of thyme, bay leaf, and parsley tied together)
- 1 cup pearl onions (or one large onion, chopped)
- 1 cup mushrooms, sliced
- 2 tbsp unsalted butter
- 1 tbsp fresh parsley, chopped (for garnish)

Instructions

1. **Prepare the Beef:**
   - Season beef cubes generously with salt and pepper.
   - Preheat your oven to 325°F (165°C).
2. **Brown the Beef:**
   - Heat vegetable oil in a large Dutch oven or heavy oven-safe pot over medium-high heat.
   - Add beef in batches to avoid overcrowding, and brown on all sides. Remove beef and set aside.
3. **Cook the Bacon:**
   - In the same pot, add diced bacon or pancetta. Cook until crispy. Remove with a slotted spoon and set aside with the beef.
4. **Sauté Vegetables:**
   - Add onions and carrots to the pot. Cook until softened, about 5-7 minutes.
   - Add garlic and cook for an additional minute.
5. **Add Flour:**
   - Stir in the flour and cook for 2 minutes to create a roux.
6. **Deglaze and Simmer:**
   - Pour in the red wine, scraping up any browned bits from the bottom of the pot. Bring to a simmer and cook for 5 minutes to reduce slightly.

- Stir in beef broth and tomato paste. Add the bouquet garni.
7. **Combine and Braise:**
    - Return the browned beef and bacon to the pot. The liquid should cover the meat about 2/3 of the way.
    - Bring to a simmer, cover, and transfer to the preheated oven. Braise for 2.5 to 3 hours, or until the meat is tender.
8. **Cook the Mushrooms and Onions:**
    - While the beef is braising, melt butter in a skillet over medium heat. Add mushrooms and pearl onions. Sauté until golden brown, about 10 minutes. Set aside.
9. **Add Mushrooms and Onions:**
    - After the beef has braised, add the mushrooms and onions to the pot. Simmer on the stove for an additional 15 minutes to combine the flavors.
10. **Finish and Serve:**
    - Remove the bouquet garni and adjust seasoning with salt and pepper.
    - Garnish with chopped parsley.

Serve Beef Bourguignon over mashed potatoes, buttered noodles, or with crusty bread. Enjoy!

BBQ Ribs

Ingredients

For the Ribs:

- 2 racks of baby back ribs (about 2-3 lbs each)
- Salt and freshly ground black pepper
- 2 tbsp olive oil

For the Dry Rub:

- 1/4 cup brown sugar
- 1 tbsp paprika
- 1 tbsp smoked paprika
- 1 tbsp garlic powder
- 1 tbsp onion powder
- 1 tsp chili powder
- 1 tsp ground cumin
- 1 tsp dried oregano
- 1/2 tsp cayenne pepper (optional, for heat)

For the BBQ Sauce:

- 1 cup barbecue sauce (your favorite brand or homemade)

Instructions

1. **Prepare the Ribs:**
   - **Remove the Membrane:** Place the ribs on a cutting board, bone-side up. Use a knife to loosen the membrane covering the back of the ribs. Grab it with a paper towel and peel it off completely. This helps make the ribs more tender.
   - **Season:** Rub the ribs with olive oil. Season generously with salt and pepper.
2. **Apply the Dry Rub:**
   - In a small bowl, mix together all the dry rub ingredients.
   - Rub the mixture evenly over both sides of the ribs. For best results, let the ribs sit with the rub for at least 30 minutes, or up to overnight in the refrigerator.
3. **Cook the Ribs:**
   Oven Method:
   - Preheat your oven to 300°F (150°C).
   - Place the ribs on a rack in a baking sheet or a roasting pan. Cover with aluminum foil.

- Bake for 2.5 to 3 hours, or until the ribs are tender and the meat easily pulls away from the bone.

4. **Grill Method:**
    - Preheat your grill to medium heat.
    - Set up your grill for indirect heat by turning on only one side of the burners (for gas) or placing coals on one side of the grill (for charcoal).
    - Place the ribs bone-side down on the cooler side of the grill. Cover and cook for 2.5 to 3 hours, turning occasionally, until the ribs are tender.

5. **Add the BBQ Sauce:**
    - Preheat your grill to medium-high heat if using the grill method.
    - Brush the BBQ sauce onto the ribs during the last 20-30 minutes of cooking. If using the oven, you can do this step in the final 30 minutes of baking.
    - For a caramelized finish, you can move the ribs to the hotter side of the grill or under the broiler for a few minutes, watching carefully to avoid burning.

6. **Rest and Serve:**
    - Remove the ribs from the oven or grill and let them rest for 5-10 minutes.
    - Cut between the bones to separate the ribs.
    - Serve with extra BBQ sauce on the side.

Enjoy your BBQ Ribs with classic sides like coleslaw, baked beans, or corn on the cob!

Roast Leg of Lamb

Ingredients

- 1 (5-6 lbs) bone-in leg of lamb
- Salt and freshly ground black pepper
- 3 tbsp olive oil
- 4 cloves garlic, minced
- 2 tbsp fresh rosemary, chopped (or 2 tsp dried rosemary)
- 2 tbsp fresh thyme, chopped (or 2 tsp dried thyme)
- 1 tbsp Dijon mustard
- 1 cup red wine (optional)
- 1 cup chicken broth
- 1 tbsp all-purpose flour (optional, for gravy)

Instructions

1. **Prepare the Lamb:**
    - Preheat your oven to 400°F (200°C).
    - Pat the leg of lamb dry with paper towels. Season generously with salt and pepper.
2. **Make the Herb Paste:**
    - In a small bowl, combine olive oil, minced garlic, chopped rosemary, chopped thyme, and Dijon mustard. Mix well to form a paste.
3. **Apply the Herb Paste:**
    - Rub the herb paste all over the leg of lamb, making sure it is well coated.
4. **Roast the Lamb:**
    - Place the lamb in a roasting pan or on a rack in a baking sheet.
    - Roast in the preheated oven for 20 minutes to develop a crust.
    - Reduce the oven temperature to 325°F (165°C) and continue roasting for approximately 1.5 to 2 hours, or until the internal temperature reaches your desired level of doneness:
        - **Medium-Rare:** 125°F (52°C)
        - **Medium:** 135°F (57°C)
        - **Medium-Well:** 145°F (63°C)
    - Use a meat thermometer to check the temperature.
5. **Rest the Lamb:**
    - Remove the lamb from the oven and let it rest for at least 15 minutes before carving. This allows the juices to redistribute and keeps the meat tender.
6. **Make the Gravy (Optional):**
    - If you'd like gravy, place the roasting pan on the stove over medium heat.

- Add red wine and chicken broth, scraping up any browned bits from the bottom of the pan.
- Bring to a simmer and cook until reduced slightly, about 5-10 minutes.
- For a thicker gravy, mix 1 tbsp flour with a little water to make a slurry, and stir into the simmering liquid. Cook until thickened.

7. **Serve:**
   - Slice the roast leg of lamb and serve with the gravy, if desired. It pairs well with roasted vegetables, potatoes, or a fresh salad.

Enjoy your Roast Leg of Lamb!

Spaghetti Bolognese

Ingredients

For the Bolognese Sauce:

- 2 tbsp olive oil
- 1 onion, finely chopped
- 2 cloves garlic, minced
- 1 carrot, peeled and finely chopped
- 1 celery stalk, finely chopped
- 1 lb (450 g) ground beef (or a mix of beef and pork)
- 1/2 cup red wine (optional)
- 1 can (14.5 oz) crushed tomatoes
- 2 tbsp tomato paste
- 1 cup beef broth
- 1 tsp dried oregano
- 1 tsp dried basil
- 1/2 tsp dried thyme
- 1/4 tsp red pepper flakes (optional, for heat)
- 1 bay leaf
- Salt and freshly ground black pepper, to taste
- 1/2 cup whole milk or heavy cream (optional, for richness)

For the Spaghetti:

- 12 oz (340 g) spaghetti
- Salt, for the pasta water
- Freshly grated Parmesan cheese (for serving)
- Fresh basil or parsley, chopped (for garnish, optional)

Instructions

1. **Prepare the Bolognese Sauce:**
    - **Sauté Vegetables:** Heat olive oil in a large skillet or Dutch oven over medium heat. Add the onion, garlic, carrot, and celery. Cook until vegetables are softened, about 5-7 minutes.
    - **Brown the Meat:** Add the ground beef (and pork, if using) to the skillet. Cook until browned, breaking it up with a spoon as it cooks. Drain excess fat if necessary.
    - **Deglaze and Simmer:** If using red wine, pour it into the skillet and cook for 2-3 minutes to reduce slightly. Stir in the crushed tomatoes, tomato paste, beef broth, oregano, basil, thyme, red pepper flakes (if using), and bay leaf. Mix well.

- **Simmer:** Bring to a simmer, reduce heat to low, and cover. Let the sauce cook gently for 30-45 minutes, stirring occasionally. If the sauce becomes too thick, add a little water or additional beef broth. For a richer sauce, stir in the milk or cream during the last 10 minutes of cooking.
- **Season:** Remove the bay leaf. Season the sauce with salt and pepper to taste.
2. **Cook the Spaghetti:**
    - While the sauce is simmering, bring a large pot of salted water to a boil. Add the spaghetti and cook according to the package instructions until al dente. Reserve 1/2 cup of pasta cooking water, then drain the pasta.
3. **Combine Pasta and Sauce:**
    - Toss the cooked spaghetti with the Bolognese sauce, adding a little reserved pasta water if needed to help the sauce coat the pasta evenly.
4. **Serve:**
    - Serve the Spaghetti Bolognese hot, garnished with freshly grated Parmesan cheese and chopped basil or parsley, if desired.

Enjoy your Spaghetti Bolognese!

Pork Schnitzel

Ingredients

- 4 pork loin chops (about 1/2 inch thick)
- Salt and freshly ground black pepper
- 1 cup all-purpose flour
- 2 large eggs
- 1 cup breadcrumbs (preferably plain or seasoned)
- 1/2 cup grated Parmesan cheese (optional)
- 1/2 tsp paprika (optional)
- 1/2 tsp garlic powder (optional)
- 1/4 cup vegetable oil (for frying)
- Lemon wedges (for serving)
- Fresh parsley, chopped (for garnish, optional)

Instructions

1. **Prepare the Pork:**
    - Place the pork loin chops between two sheets of plastic wrap or parchment paper.
    - Use a meat mallet or rolling pin to pound the pork chops to an even thickness of about 1/4 inch. This ensures they cook evenly and stay tender.
2. **Season the Pork:**
    - Season both sides of the pork chops with salt and pepper.
3. **Set Up a Breading Station:**
    - Place the flour in a shallow dish.
    - In another shallow dish, beat the eggs.
    - In a third shallow dish, combine the breadcrumbs, Parmesan cheese (if using), paprika, and garlic powder.
4. **Bread the Pork:**
    - Dredge each pork chop in the flour, shaking off the excess.
    - Dip into the beaten eggs, allowing any excess to drip off.
    - Coat thoroughly with the breadcrumb mixture, pressing the breadcrumbs onto the pork to adhere well.
5. **Fry the Schnitzels:**
    - Heat vegetable oil in a large skillet over medium-high heat. You need enough oil to cover the bottom of the pan and come up about 1/4 inch.
    - Add the pork chops to the skillet in batches, being careful not to overcrowd the pan.

- Fry the schnitzels for about 3-4 minutes per side, or until golden brown and crispy. The internal temperature should reach 145°F (63°C). Adjust heat as needed to avoid burning the breadcrumbs.
6. **Drain and Serve:**
    - Transfer the cooked schnitzels to a paper towel-lined plate to drain excess oil.
    - Serve immediately with lemon wedges for squeezing over the top. Garnish with chopped fresh parsley if desired.

Serving Suggestions:

- Pork Schnitzel pairs well with a variety of sides such as potato salad, cucumber salad, or a fresh green salad.
- Traditional accompaniments include a simple lemon wedge and maybe some lingonberry jam.

Enjoy your Pork Schnitzel!

Moroccan Lamb Tagine

Ingredients

- 2 lbs (900 g) lamb shoulder or leg, cut into 1.5-inch cubes
- Salt and freshly ground black pepper
- 2 tbsp olive oil
- 1 large onion, chopped
- 3 cloves garlic, minced
- 1 tbsp ground cumin
- 1 tbsp ground coriander
- 1 tbsp ground paprika
- 1 tsp ground cinnamon
- 1/2 tsp ground turmeric
- 1/4 tsp ground cayenne pepper (optional, for heat)
- 1/2 cup dried apricots, chopped
- 1/2 cup green olives, pitted and sliced
- 1 can (14.5 oz) diced tomatoes
- 2 cups chicken or beef broth
- 1/2 cup almonds, toasted (optional)
- 2 tbsp honey
- 1 cup chickpeas (canned or cooked)
- 1/2 cup fresh cilantro or parsley, chopped (for garnish)
- Cooked couscous or rice (for serving)

Instructions

1. **Prepare the Lamb:**
    - Season the lamb cubes generously with salt and pepper.
2. **Sear the Lamb:**
    - Heat olive oil in a large tagine or Dutch oven over medium-high heat.
    - Add the lamb in batches to avoid overcrowding, and brown on all sides. Remove the browned lamb and set aside.
3. **Sauté Vegetables:**
    - In the same pot, add chopped onion. Cook until softened and translucent, about 5-7 minutes.
    - Add minced garlic and cook for an additional minute.
4. **Add Spices:**
    - Stir in ground cumin, coriander, paprika, cinnamon, turmeric, and cayenne pepper (if using). Cook for 1-2 minutes until fragrant.
5. **Combine Ingredients:**
    - Return the browned lamb to the pot.

- Stir in chopped dried apricots, green olives, diced tomatoes, and broth. Mix well.
6. **Simmer the Tagine:**
    - Bring to a boil, then reduce heat to low. Cover and simmer gently for 1.5 to 2 hours, or until the lamb is tender and easily pulls apart. Stir occasionally and add more broth if necessary.
7. **Finish the Tagine:**
    - Stir in honey and chickpeas. Simmer for another 10-15 minutes to heat through and allow the flavors to meld.
8. **Garnish and Serve:**
    - Adjust seasoning with salt and pepper as needed.
    - Garnish with toasted almonds (if using) and chopped fresh cilantro or parsley.
    - Serve the tagine hot over cooked couscous or rice.

Enjoy your Moroccan Lamb Tagine!

Veal Parmesan

Ingredients

For the Veal:

- 4 veal cutlets (about 1/2 inch thick)
- Salt and freshly ground black pepper
- 1 cup all-purpose flour
- 2 large eggs
- 1 cup breadcrumbs (preferably plain or seasoned)
- 1/2 cup grated Parmesan cheese
- 1/2 tsp garlic powder (optional)
- 1/2 tsp dried oregano (optional)
- 1/4 cup vegetable oil (for frying)

For the Tomato Sauce:

- 2 cups marinara sauce (store-bought or homemade)
- 1 cup shredded mozzarella cheese
- 1/2 cup grated Parmesan cheese
- Fresh basil or parsley, chopped (for garnish)

Instructions

1. **Prepare the Veal:**
    - Season veal cutlets with salt and pepper on both sides.
2. **Set Up a Breading Station:**
    - Place the flour in a shallow dish.
    - In another shallow dish, beat the eggs.
    - In a third shallow dish, combine breadcrumbs, grated Parmesan cheese, garlic powder, and dried oregano (if using).
3. **Bread the Veal:**
    - Dredge each veal cutlet in flour, shaking off the excess.
    - Dip into the beaten eggs, allowing any excess to drip off.
    - Coat thoroughly with the breadcrumb mixture, pressing the breadcrumbs onto the veal to adhere well.
4. **Fry the Veal:**
    - Heat vegetable oil in a large skillet over medium-high heat.
    - Add veal cutlets and cook for about 2-3 minutes per side, or until golden brown and cooked through. Remove from the skillet and set aside on a paper towel-lined plate to drain excess oil.
5. **Preheat Oven:**

    - Preheat your oven to 375°F (190°C).
6. **Assemble the Dish:**
    - Spread a thin layer of marinara sauce on the bottom of a baking dish.
    - Place the fried veal cutlets in the baking dish.
    - Spoon additional marinara sauce over each cutlet.
    - Sprinkle shredded mozzarella cheese and grated Parmesan cheese on top of the veal.
7. **Bake:**
    - Bake in the preheated oven for about 15-20 minutes, or until the cheese is melted and bubbly, and the sauce is heated through.
8. **Garnish and Serve:**
    - Garnish with chopped fresh basil or parsley.
    - Serve hot with a side of pasta, a green salad, or garlic bread.

Enjoy your Veal Parmesan!

Beef Empanadas

Ingredients

For the Filling:

- 1 lb (450 g) ground beef
- 1 tbsp olive oil
- 1 onion, finely chopped
- 2 cloves garlic, minced
- 1 bell pepper (red or green), finely chopped
- 1/2 cup black olives, chopped (optional)
- 1/2 cup raisins (optional)
- 2 tsp ground cumin
- 1 tsp smoked paprika
- 1/2 tsp ground cinnamon
- 1/4 tsp ground cloves
- Salt and freshly ground black pepper, to taste
- 1/4 cup tomato paste
- 1/2 cup beef or chicken broth
- 1/4 cup fresh cilantro or parsley, chopped (for garnish)

For the Dough:

- 2 1/2 cups all-purpose flour
- 1/2 tsp salt
- 1/2 cup unsalted butter, chilled and cubed
- 1 large egg
- 1/2 cup cold water (adjust as needed)

For Assembling:

- 1 egg, beaten (for egg wash)

Instructions

1. **Prepare the Filling:**
    - **Cook the Beef:** Heat olive oil in a large skillet over medium heat. Add the ground beef and cook until browned, breaking it up with a spoon. Drain excess fat if necessary.
    - **Sauté Vegetables:** Add the chopped onion, garlic, and bell pepper to the skillet. Cook until vegetables are softened, about 5 minutes.

- **Season:** Stir in the black olives, raisins, cumin, smoked paprika, cinnamon, cloves, salt, and pepper. Cook for another 2 minutes.
    - **Add Tomato Paste and Broth:** Stir in the tomato paste and cook for 2 minutes. Add the beef or chicken broth and simmer until the mixture is thickened, about 5-7 minutes. Remove from heat and let cool. Stir in fresh cilantro or parsley.
2. **Prepare the Dough:**
    - **Mix Dry Ingredients:** In a large bowl, whisk together the flour and salt.
    - **Cut in Butter:** Add the chilled, cubed butter. Use a pastry cutter or your fingers to cut the butter into the flour until the mixture resembles coarse crumbs.
    - **Add Egg and Water:** Beat the egg and add it to the flour mixture. Gradually add cold water, mixing until a dough forms. You may need slightly more or less water, so add it gradually.
    - **Chill Dough:** Turn the dough onto a lightly floured surface, knead a few times to bring it together, then wrap in plastic wrap and refrigerate for at least 30 minutes.
3. **Assemble the Empanadas:**
    - **Preheat Oven:** Preheat your oven to 375°F (190°C).
    - **Roll Out Dough:** On a floured surface, roll out the dough to about 1/8 inch thickness. Cut into 4-5 inch circles using a cookie cutter or a glass.
    - **Fill and Seal:** Place a spoonful of the cooled beef filling in the center of each dough circle. Fold the dough over to form a half-moon shape and crimp the edges with a fork to seal. Alternatively, use a crimper or your fingers to seal the edges.
    - **Egg Wash:** Place the filled empanadas on a baking sheet lined with parchment paper. Brush the tops with the beaten egg.
4. **Bake:**
    - Bake for 20-25 minutes, or until the empanadas are golden brown and crispy.
5. **Serve:**
    - Let the empanadas cool slightly before serving. They are great as an appetizer, snack, or main dish.

Enjoy your Beef Empanadas!

Duck Confit

Ingredients

- 4 duck legs (thigh and drumstick)
- Salt (for curing)
- 4 cloves garlic, minced
- 2 sprigs fresh thyme
- 1 bay leaf
- 2 cups duck fat (or enough to cover the duck legs)
- Freshly ground black pepper

Instructions

1. **Cure the Duck:**
    - **Season:** Pat the duck legs dry with paper towels. Generously season all sides of the duck legs with salt. Place the duck legs in a single layer in a dish.
    - **Add Aromatics:** Sprinkle the minced garlic over the duck legs. Place the thyme sprigs and bay leaf on top.
    - **Cure:** Cover the dish with plastic wrap and refrigerate for at least 24 hours, or up to 48 hours. This step allows the salt to penetrate the meat and enhances flavor.
2. **Rinse and Dry:**
    - **Rinse:** After curing, rinse the duck legs under cold water to remove excess salt and pat them dry with paper towels.
3. **Cook the Duck:**
    - **Preheat Oven:** Preheat your oven to 275°F (135°C).
    - **Heat Duck Fat:** In a large oven-safe pot or Dutch oven, melt the duck fat over low heat. You want the fat to be warm but not hot.
    - **Add Duck Legs:** Submerge the duck legs in the warm duck fat. The legs should be completely covered. If necessary, add more duck fat to ensure the legs are fully immersed.
    - **Cook:** Place the pot in the preheated oven and cook for 2.5 to 3 hours, or until the duck is tender and the meat easily pulls away from the bone.
4. **Finish and Serve:**
    - **Crisp the Skin:** If desired, after cooking, you can crisp the skin by placing the duck legs under a broiler for 5-7 minutes, or until the skin is crispy and browned. Watch closely to prevent burning.
    - **Serve:** Serve the duck confit with your favorite sides, such as roasted potatoes, sautéed greens, or a simple salad. Duck confit pairs well with a variety of sides and is often enjoyed with a rich sauce or fruit preserves.
5. **Storing Leftovers:**

- **Store:** Any leftover duck confit can be stored in the duck fat in an airtight container in the refrigerator for up to 2 weeks. To reheat, gently warm the duck legs in the fat or crisp the skin under a broiler.

Enjoy your Duck Confit!

Meatloaf

Ingredients

- 1 lb (450 g) ground beef
- 1/2 lb (225 g) ground pork
- 1 cup breadcrumbs
- 1/2 cup milk
- 1/2 cup ketchup
- 1/4 cup finely chopped onion
- 2 cloves garlic, minced
- 1 large egg
- 2 tbsp Worcestershire sauce
- 1 tbsp Dijon mustard
- 1 tsp dried thyme
- 1 tsp dried oregano
- Salt and freshly ground black pepper, to taste

For the Glaze:

- 1/4 cup ketchup
- 2 tbsp brown sugar
- 1 tbsp Dijon mustard

Instructions

1. **Preheat Oven:**
    - Preheat your oven to 375°F (190°C).
2. **Prepare the Meat Mixture:**
    - In a large bowl, combine ground beef, ground pork, breadcrumbs, milk, ketchup, chopped onion, minced garlic, egg, Worcestershire sauce, Dijon mustard, dried thyme, dried oregano, salt, and pepper. Mix until all ingredients are well combined, but do not overmix.
3. **Shape the Meatloaf:**
    - Transfer the meat mixture to a baking sheet or a loaf pan. Shape into a loaf about 8-10 inches long. If using a baking sheet, you may want to line it with parchment paper or lightly grease it.
4. **Prepare the Glaze:**
    - In a small bowl, mix together ketchup, brown sugar, and Dijon mustard.
5. **Bake:**
    - Brush the glaze over the top of the meatloaf.

- Bake in the preheated oven for about 60-75 minutes, or until the internal temperature of the meatloaf reaches 160°F (71°C) and the top is caramelized and slightly crispy.
6. **Rest and Serve:**
    - Allow the meatloaf to rest for 10 minutes before slicing. This helps the juices redistribute and makes for cleaner slices.
    - Serve with your favorite side dishes, such as mashed potatoes, steamed vegetables, or a simple salad.

Enjoy your classic meatloaf!

Beef Tacos

Ingredients

For the Beef Filling:

- 1 lb (450 g) ground beef
- 1 tbsp olive oil
- 1 small onion, finely chopped
- 2 cloves garlic, minced
- 1 bell pepper (red or green), finely chopped
- 1 packet (1 oz) taco seasoning mix (or homemade seasoning, see below)
- 1/2 cup tomato sauce or diced tomatoes
- 1/2 cup beef broth
- Salt and freshly ground black pepper, to taste

For Homemade Taco Seasoning (optional):

- 1 tbsp chili powder
- 1 tsp ground cumin
- 1 tsp paprika
- 1/2 tsp garlic powder
- 1/2 tsp onion powder
- 1/2 tsp dried oregano
- 1/4 tsp cayenne pepper (optional, for heat)
- Salt and pepper to taste

For Assembling:

- Taco shells or tortillas (soft or crunchy)
- Shredded lettuce
- Diced tomatoes
- Shredded cheese (cheddar, Monterey Jack, or your choice)
- Sour cream
- Salsa
- Sliced jalapeños (optional)
- Chopped cilantro (optional)
- Lime wedges (for serving)

Instructions

1. **Cook the Beef Filling:**
    - **Heat Oil:** In a large skillet, heat the olive oil over medium heat.

- **Sauté Vegetables:** Add the chopped onion and bell pepper. Cook until softened, about 5 minutes. Add the minced garlic and cook for another 1 minute.
   - **Brown the Beef:** Add the ground beef to the skillet. Cook until browned, breaking it up with a spoon as it cooks. Drain any excess fat if necessary.
   - **Add Seasoning:** Stir in the taco seasoning mix (or homemade seasoning) and tomato sauce or diced tomatoes. Mix well.
   - **Simmer:** Add the beef broth and bring to a simmer. Reduce heat and let it cook for 5-10 minutes, or until the sauce has thickened slightly. Season with salt and pepper to taste.
2. **Prepare Taco Shells or Tortillas:**
   - **Crunchy Shells:** If using store-bought crunchy taco shells, follow package instructions to heat them up.
   - **Soft Tortillas:** If using tortillas, you can warm them in a dry skillet over medium heat for about 30 seconds per side or wrap them in a damp paper towel and microwave for about 20-30 seconds.
3. **Assemble the Tacos:**
   - Spoon the cooked beef mixture into each taco shell or tortilla.
   - Top with your favorite toppings such as shredded lettuce, diced tomatoes, shredded cheese, sour cream, salsa, sliced jalapeños, and chopped cilantro.
   - Serve with lime wedges on the side.

Enjoy your Beef Tacos!

Chicken Fried Steak

Ingredients

For the Steak:

- 4 beef cube steaks (about 1/2 inch thick)
- Salt and freshly ground black pepper
- 1 cup all-purpose flour
- 1 tsp garlic powder
- 1 tsp onion powder
- 1/2 tsp paprika
- 1/2 tsp dried thyme
- 2 large eggs
- 1 cup buttermilk (or regular milk with 1 tbsp lemon juice or vinegar)
- Vegetable oil (for frying)

For the Gravy:

- 2 tbsp vegetable oil (from frying)
- 2 tbsp all-purpose flour
- 2 cups milk
- Salt and freshly ground black pepper, to taste

Instructions

1. **Prepare the Steak:**
   - **Tenderize and Season:** Pat the cube steaks dry with paper towels. Season both sides with salt and pepper.
   - **Set Up Breading Station:** In one shallow dish, combine flour, garlic powder, onion powder, paprika, and dried thyme. In another dish, beat the eggs and mix with buttermilk.
2. **Bread the Steak:**
   - **Dredge in Flour:** Dredge each steak in the seasoned flour, shaking off the excess.
   - **Dip in Buttermilk:** Dip the floured steak into the buttermilk mixture, letting excess drip off.
   - **Coat Again in Flour:** Return the steak to the flour mixture, pressing the flour onto the steak to coat well.
3. **Fry the Steak:**
   - **Heat Oil:** Heat about 1/2 inch of vegetable oil in a large skillet over medium-high heat. The oil should be hot but not smoking.

- **Fry:** Fry the steaks in batches (don't overcrowd the pan), cooking for 3-4 minutes per side, or until golden brown and crispy. The internal temperature should reach 145°F (63°C). Adjust heat as needed to avoid burning the coating.
- **Drain:** Transfer the fried steaks to a paper towel-lined plate to drain excess oil.

4. **Make the Gravy:**
   - **Prepare Roux:** In the same skillet, remove excess oil, leaving about 2 tablespoons in the pan. Add 2 tablespoons of flour to the pan and cook over medium heat, stirring constantly, until the flour is lightly browned (about 2-3 minutes).
   - **Add Milk:** Gradually whisk in the milk, making sure to scrape up any browned bits from the bottom of the pan. Continue to cook and whisk until the gravy thickens, about 5-7 minutes.
   - **Season:** Season with salt and pepper to taste.

5. **Serve:**
   - **Serve:** Pour the gravy over the fried steaks or serve it on the side. Chicken Fried Steak is typically enjoyed with mashed potatoes, green beans, or other classic sides.

Enjoy your Chicken Fried Steak!

Pork Belly Buns

Ingredients

For the Pork Belly:

- 2 lbs (900 g) pork belly, skin-on
- 1 tbsp salt
- 1 tbsp sugar
- 1 tbsp Chinese five-spice powder
- 2 cloves garlic, minced
- 1 inch ginger, minced
- 1/4 cup soy sauce
- 1/4 cup hoisin sauce
- 1/4 cup rice vinegar
- 1 tbsp sesame oil
- 1/2 cup water

For the Buns:

- 12 steamed bao buns (store-bought or homemade)
- 1/4 cup hoisin sauce (for spreading)
- 1/2 cup pickled cucumbers (recipe below or store-bought)
- 1/2 cup shredded carrots
- 1/4 cup fresh cilantro leaves
- 1-2 green onions, sliced

For Pickled Cucumbers (Optional):

- 1 cup thinly sliced cucumber
- 1/4 cup rice vinegar
- 2 tbsp sugar
- 1/2 tsp salt

Instructions

1. **Prepare the Pork Belly:**
    - **Preheat Oven:** Preheat your oven to 300°F (150°C).
    - **Season:** Pat the pork belly dry with paper towels. Rub the skin with salt and sugar. Mix the Chinese five-spice powder, minced garlic, and minced ginger. Rub this mixture all over the pork belly.

- **Roast:** Place the pork belly in a roasting pan, skin-side up. Mix soy sauce, hoisin sauce, rice vinegar, sesame oil, and water in a bowl and pour over the pork belly. Cover the pan with aluminum foil.
- **Cook:** Roast in the preheated oven for 2.5 to 3 hours, or until the pork belly is tender. Remove the foil in the last 30 minutes to allow the skin to crisp up.

2. **Make the Pickled Cucumbers (Optional):**
   - **Pickle:** In a bowl, combine rice vinegar, sugar, and salt. Stir until sugar and salt are dissolved. Add the sliced cucumber and let sit for at least 30 minutes. For quicker pickling, you can refrigerate the cucumbers for a few hours.
3. **Prepare the Bao Buns:**
   - **Steam Buns:** Steam the bao buns according to package instructions or using a steamer basket over boiling water. Keep them warm until ready to use.
4. **Assemble the Buns:**
   - **Slice Pork Belly:** Once the pork belly is done, let it rest for about 10 minutes. Slice it into small pieces or bite-sized chunks.
   - **Spread Sauce:** Spread a thin layer of hoisin sauce inside each steamed bao bun.
   - **Add Pork:** Place a few pieces of the sliced pork belly inside each bun.
   - **Add Toppings:** Top with pickled cucumbers, shredded carrots, fresh cilantro leaves, and sliced green onions.
5. **Serve:**
   - Serve the pork belly buns warm and enjoy!

These Pork Belly Buns are perfect for a tasty appetizer, party snack, or even a fun meal. Enjoy!

Beef and Ale Pie

Ingredients

For the Filling:

- 1.5 lbs (680 g) beef chuck or stewing beef, cut into 1-inch cubes
- 2 tbsp olive oil
- 1 large onion, finely chopped
- 2 cloves garlic, minced
- 2 large carrots, diced
- 2 celery stalks, diced
- 2 tbsp tomato paste
- 2 tbsp all-purpose flour
- 1 cup (240 ml) ale or stout (dark beer)
- 1 cup (240 ml) beef broth
- 2 tsp dried thyme
- 1 bay leaf
- Salt and freshly ground black pepper, to taste
- 1 cup (150 g) frozen peas (optional)

For the Pie Crust:

- 2 1/2 cups (315 g) all-purpose flour
- 1/2 tsp salt
- 1 cup (225 g) unsalted butter, chilled and cut into cubes
- 6-8 tbsp cold water

For the Topping:

- 1 egg, beaten (for egg wash)
- Fresh parsley, chopped (for garnish, optional)

Instructions

1. **Prepare the Filling:**
   - **Brown the Beef:** Heat olive oil in a large skillet or Dutch oven over medium-high heat. Add the beef cubes in batches, browning them on all sides. Remove the beef and set aside.
   - **Sauté Vegetables:** In the same pot, add the onion, garlic, carrots, and celery. Cook until the vegetables are softened, about 5-7 minutes.

- **Add Tomato Paste and Flour:** Stir in the tomato paste and cook for 2 minutes. Sprinkle the flour over the vegetables and cook for another 2 minutes, stirring constantly.
- **Add Liquids and Seasoning:** Gradually add the ale and beef broth, stirring to combine. Add the browned beef, thyme, bay leaf, salt, and pepper. Bring to a simmer.
- **Simmer:** Reduce the heat to low, cover, and let simmer for 1.5 to 2 hours, or until the beef is tender and the sauce has thickened. If using, stir in the frozen peas during the last 10 minutes of cooking. Remove the bay leaf and adjust seasoning as needed. Let the filling cool slightly.

2. **Prepare the Pie Crust:**
   - **Mix Dry Ingredients:** In a large bowl, whisk together flour and salt.
   - **Cut in Butter:** Add chilled butter cubes and use a pastry cutter or your fingers to work the butter into the flour until the mixture resembles coarse crumbs.
   - **Add Water:** Gradually add cold water, 1 tablespoon at a time, mixing until the dough comes together. You may need slightly more or less water.
   - **Chill Dough:** Divide the dough into two portions (one slightly larger for the base). Shape each portion into a disc, wrap in plastic wrap, and refrigerate for at least 30 minutes.

3. **Assemble the Pie:**
   - **Preheat Oven:** Preheat your oven to 375°F (190°C).
   - **Roll Out Dough:** On a lightly floured surface, roll out the larger portion of dough to fit a 9-inch pie dish. Place it in the dish and trim the edges.
   - **Add Filling:** Spoon the beef filling into the pie crust.
   - **Top with Crust:** Roll out the remaining dough and place it over the filling. Trim and crimp the edges to seal. Cut a few slits in the top crust to allow steam to escape.
   - **Apply Egg Wash:** Brush the top crust with the beaten egg.

4. **Bake:**
   - Bake in the preheated oven for 35-40 minutes, or until the crust is golden brown and the filling is bubbling.

5. **Serve:**
   - Let the pie cool for about 10 minutes before serving. Garnish with chopped fresh parsley if desired.

Enjoy your Beef and Ale Pie!

Chicken Alfredo

Ingredients

For the Chicken:

- 2 large boneless, skinless chicken breasts (or 4 smaller ones)
- Salt and freshly ground black pepper
- 2 tbsp olive oil
- 1 tsp garlic powder (optional)
- 1 tsp onion powder (optional)

For the Alfredo Sauce:

- 4 tbsp unsalted butter
- 3 cloves garlic, minced
- 1 cup heavy cream
- 1 cup (100 g) grated Parmesan cheese
- 1/2 cup (120 ml) chicken broth
- 1/4 tsp ground nutmeg (optional)
- Salt and freshly ground black pepper, to taste

For Serving:

- 12 oz (340 g) fettuccine pasta (or your choice of pasta)
- Fresh parsley, chopped (for garnish, optional)

Instructions

1. **Cook the Pasta:**
   - **Boil Water:** Bring a large pot of salted water to a boil.
   - **Cook Pasta:** Add the fettuccine and cook according to package instructions until al dente. Reserve 1/2 cup of pasta water, then drain the pasta and set aside.
2. **Prepare the Chicken:**
   - **Season:** Season the chicken breasts with salt, pepper, garlic powder, and onion powder (if using).
   - **Cook Chicken:** Heat olive oil in a large skillet over medium-high heat. Add the chicken breasts and cook for about 6-7 minutes per side, or until golden brown and cooked through (internal temperature should reach 165°F or 74°C). Remove from the skillet and let rest for a few minutes before slicing.
3. **Make the Alfredo Sauce:**
   - **Sauté Garlic:** In the same skillet used for the chicken, melt the butter over medium heat. Add the minced garlic and sauté for about 1 minute, until fragrant.

- **Add Cream and Broth:** Pour in the heavy cream and chicken broth. Bring to a simmer and cook for 2-3 minutes, allowing it to reduce slightly.
    - **Add Cheese:** Stir in the grated Parmesan cheese and cook, stirring constantly, until the cheese is melted and the sauce is smooth. Season with salt, pepper, and ground nutmeg (if using). Adjust seasoning to taste.
4. **Combine Pasta and Sauce:**
    - **Add Pasta:** Toss the cooked pasta into the Alfredo sauce, adding a little reserved pasta water if needed to reach your desired sauce consistency.
    - **Slice Chicken:** Slice the cooked chicken breasts into strips and place them on top of the pasta. Alternatively, you can mix the chicken into the pasta if preferred.
5. **Serve:**
    - **Garnish:** Garnish with chopped fresh parsley if desired.
    - **Serve:** Serve immediately while hot.

Enjoy your creamy Chicken Alfredo!

Grilled Ribeye Steak

Ingredients

- 2 ribeye steaks (about 1.5 inches thick, 12-16 oz each)
- 2 tbsp olive oil
- Salt and freshly ground black pepper, to taste
- 2 cloves garlic, minced (optional)
- 1 tsp dried rosemary or thyme (optional)
- 1 tbsp butter (optional, for finishing)
- Fresh herbs (rosemary or thyme, for garnish, optional)

Instructions

1. **Prepare the Steaks:**
    - **Season:** Pat the ribeye steaks dry with paper towels. Rub both sides with olive oil. Season generously with salt and freshly ground black pepper. For added flavor, you can also rub the steaks with minced garlic and dried rosemary or thyme if using.
    - **Rest:** Let the steaks sit at room temperature for about 30 minutes to ensure even cooking.
2. **Preheat the Grill:**
    - **Heat Grill:** Preheat your grill to high heat (about 450-500°F or 230-260°C). If using a charcoal grill, ensure the coals are hot and ashed over. If using a gas grill, turn all burners on high.
3. **Grill the Steaks:**
    - **Grill:** Place the steaks on the grill. Close the lid and cook for about 4-5 minutes per side for medium-rare. Adjust the time based on your preferred doneness:
        - **Rare:** 120-125°F (49-52°C), about 3-4 minutes per side
        - **Medium-Rare:** 130-135°F (54-57°C), about 4-5 minutes per side
        - **Medium:** 140-145°F (60-63°C), about 5-6 minutes per side
        - **Medium-Well:** 150-155°F (66-68°C), about 6-7 minutes per side
        - **Well-Done:** 160°F+ (71°C+), about 7-8 minutes per side
4. **Check for Doneness:**
    - **Use a Thermometer:** For best results, use an instant-read meat thermometer to check the internal temperature of the steaks.
5. **Rest the Steaks:**
    - **Rest:** Remove the steaks from the grill and transfer them to a cutting board. Let them rest for about 5-10 minutes to allow the juices to redistribute.
6. **Finish and Serve:**
    - **Optional Butter:** For extra flavor, you can top each steak with a pat of butter during the resting period.

- **Garnish:** Garnish with fresh herbs if desired.
- **Serve:** Slice against the grain and serve with your favorite sides, such as grilled vegetables, baked potatoes, or a fresh salad.

Enjoy your perfectly grilled Ribeye Steak!

Shrimp and Grits

Ingredients

For the Grits:

- 1 cup stone-ground grits
- 4 cups water (or chicken broth for more flavor)
- 1 cup milk or heavy cream
- 2 tbsp unsalted butter
- 1 cup shredded sharp cheddar cheese (optional)
- Salt and freshly ground black pepper, to taste

For the Shrimp:

- 1 lb (450 g) large shrimp, peeled and deveined
- 2 tbsp olive oil
- 4 slices bacon, chopped
- 1/2 cup onion, finely chopped
- 2 cloves garlic, minced
- 1/2 cup bell pepper, finely chopped (red or green)
- 1/2 cup chicken broth
- 1 tbsp lemon juice
- 1/2 tsp smoked paprika
- 1/4 tsp cayenne pepper (optional, for heat)
- Salt and freshly ground black pepper, to taste
- 2 green onions, sliced (for garnish)
- Fresh parsley, chopped (for garnish)

Instructions

1. **Prepare the Grits:**
   - **Cook Grits:** In a medium saucepan, bring water (or chicken broth) to a boil. Slowly whisk in the grits to prevent lumps. Reduce heat to low and cook, stirring occasionally, for 20-25 minutes, or until the grits are thick and tender.
   - **Add Milk/Cream and Cheese:** Stir in milk or heavy cream and butter. If using cheese, stir it in until melted and well combined. Season with salt and pepper to taste. Keep warm.
2. **Prepare the Shrimp:**
   - **Cook Bacon:** In a large skillet, cook the chopped bacon over medium heat until crisp. Remove bacon from the skillet and set aside, leaving the bacon drippings in the pan.

- **Sauté Vegetables:** Add olive oil to the skillet (if needed). Sauté onion and bell pepper in the bacon drippings until softened, about 5 minutes. Add garlic and cook for another 1 minute.
- **Cook Shrimp:** Add the shrimp to the skillet and cook until pink and opaque, about 2-3 minutes per side.
- **Add Flavor:** Stir in chicken broth, lemon juice, smoked paprika, cayenne pepper (if using), and cooked bacon. Cook for an additional 2 minutes, allowing the sauce to slightly reduce. Season with salt and pepper to taste.

3. **Serve:**
    - **Plate:** Spoon the creamy grits onto serving plates. Top with the shrimp and sauce.
    - **Garnish:** Sprinkle with sliced green onions and chopped fresh parsley.

Enjoy your Shrimp and Grits! This dish pairs wonderfully with a side of sautéed greens or a fresh garden salad.

Stuffed Pork Chops

Ingredients

For the Stuffed Pork Chops:

- 4 bone-in pork chops (1.5 to 2 inches thick)
- 2 tbsp olive oil
- Salt and freshly ground black pepper, to taste

For the Stuffing:

- 1 cup stale bread cubes or croutons
- 2 tbsp olive oil or unsalted butter
- 1 small onion, finely chopped
- 2 cloves garlic, minced
- 1 celery stalk, finely chopped
- 1/2 cup fresh parsley, chopped
- 1/2 tsp dried thyme
- 1/2 tsp dried rosemary
- 1/4 cup grated Parmesan cheese
- 1/4 cup chicken broth or vegetable broth
- 1 large egg, beaten

Instructions

1. **Prepare the Stuffing:**
    - **Sauté Vegetables:** In a medium skillet, heat olive oil or butter over medium heat. Add onion, garlic, and celery. Cook until vegetables are softened, about 5 minutes.
    - **Mix Stuffing:** In a bowl, combine bread cubes or croutons with the sautéed vegetables. Stir in parsley, thyme, rosemary, Parmesan cheese, and broth. Mix in the beaten egg until the mixture is evenly moistened. If too dry, add a bit more broth.
2. **Prepare the Pork Chops:**
    - **Preheat Oven:** Preheat your oven to 375°F (190°C).
    - **Prepare Chops:** Use a sharp knife to cut a pocket into each pork chop. Be careful not to cut all the way through; leave a border around the edges.
    - **Season:** Season the outside and inside of each pork chop with salt and pepper.
3. **Stuff the Pork Chops:**
    - **Fill Chops:** Spoon the stuffing mixture into each pork chop pocket. Pack it in gently but firmly. Secure the opening with toothpicks if needed.
4. **Cook the Pork Chops:**

- **Sear:** Heat olive oil in an oven-safe skillet over medium-high heat. Add the stuffed pork chops and sear for about 3-4 minutes per side, until golden brown.
- **Finish in Oven:** Transfer the skillet to the preheated oven and bake for 20-25 minutes, or until the pork reaches an internal temperature of 145°F (63°C). The stuffing should be heated through and the pork should be tender.

5. **Serve:**
   - **Rest:** Remove the pork chops from the oven and let them rest for 5 minutes before serving. This helps the juices redistribute and makes the chops more tender.
   - **Remove Toothpicks:** If you used toothpicks, carefully remove them before serving.

Serve your Stuffed Pork Chops with a side of roasted vegetables, mashed potatoes, or a simple salad for a complete meal. Enjoy!

Beef Fajitas

Ingredients

For the Beef Marinade:

- 1 lb (450 g) flank steak or skirt steak
- 1/4 cup lime juice (about 2 limes)
- 3 tbsp olive oil
- 2 cloves garlic, minced
- 1 tsp ground cumin
- 1 tsp smoked paprika
- 1/2 tsp chili powder
- 1/2 tsp dried oregano
- 1/2 tsp ground coriander
- Salt and freshly ground black pepper, to taste

For the Vegetables:

- 1 tbsp olive oil
- 1 large bell pepper, sliced (red, yellow, or green)
- 1 large onion, sliced
- 1/2 tsp ground cumin
- 1/2 tsp smoked paprika
- 1/4 tsp chili powder
- Salt and freshly ground black pepper, to taste

For Serving:

- Flour tortillas (or corn tortillas)
- Sliced avocado or guacamole
- Sour cream
- Salsa or pico de gallo
- Fresh cilantro, chopped (for garnish)
- Lime wedges (for garnish)

Instructions

1. **Marinate the Beef:**
   - **Prepare Marinade:** In a bowl, mix lime juice, olive oil, minced garlic, ground cumin, smoked paprika, chili powder, dried oregano, ground coriander, salt, and pepper.

- **Marinate Beef:** Place the flank or skirt steak in a resealable plastic bag or shallow dish. Pour the marinade over the steak, ensuring it's well coated. Seal the bag or cover the dish and refrigerate for at least 1 hour, or overnight for more flavor.
2. **Prepare the Vegetables:**
    - **Sauté Vegetables:** Heat olive oil in a large skillet over medium-high heat. Add the sliced bell pepper and onion. Sprinkle with ground cumin, smoked paprika, chili powder, salt, and pepper. Cook, stirring occasionally, until the vegetables are tender and slightly charred, about 7-10 minutes. Remove from skillet and set aside.
3. **Cook the Beef:**
    - **Preheat Skillet or Grill:** If using a skillet, heat a large skillet over medium-high heat. If using a grill, preheat it to medium-high heat.
    - **Cook Beef:** Remove the steak from the marinade and discard the marinade. If using a skillet, cook the steak for about 4-5 minutes per side for medium-rare, or longer to your desired doneness. If using a grill, cook the steak for about 4-5 minutes per side, depending on thickness and desired doneness. Use a meat thermometer to check the internal temperature: 135°F (57°C) for medium-rare.
    - **Rest and Slice:** Transfer the steak to a cutting board and let it rest for 5 minutes. Slice the steak thinly against the grain.
4. **Serve:**
    - **Warm Tortillas:** Heat the flour or corn tortillas according to package instructions or on a hot, dry skillet until warm and pliable.
    - **Assemble Fajitas:** To serve, place some sliced beef and sautéed vegetables onto each tortilla. Top with avocado or guacamole, sour cream, salsa or pico de gallo, and fresh cilantro. Squeeze a lime wedge over the top if desired.

Enjoy your homemade Beef Fajitas!

Roast Beef and Yorkshire Pudding

Ingredients:

- 4-5 lb (1.8-2.3 kg) beef rib roast or sirloin roast
- 2 tbsp olive oil
- Salt and freshly ground black pepper
- 4 cloves garlic, minced
- 2 sprigs fresh rosemary, leaves removed and chopped
- 2 sprigs fresh thyme, leaves removed and chopped
- 1 cup beef broth (or water)

Instructions:

1. **Prepare the Beef:**
   - **Season:** Preheat your oven to 450°F (230°C). Pat the beef roast dry with paper towels. Rub the roast with olive oil, salt, pepper, minced garlic, rosemary, and thyme.
   - **Roast:** Place the beef in a roasting pan, fat side up. Roast in the preheated oven for 15 minutes to sear the outside. Reduce the temperature to 325°F (165°C) and continue roasting for about 1.5 to 2 hours, or until the internal temperature reaches your desired level of doneness:
     - **Rare:** 125°F (52°C)
     - **Medium-Rare:** 135°F (57°C)
     - **Medium:** 145°F (63°C)
     - **Medium-Well:** 150°F (66°C)
     - **Well-Done:** 160°F (71°C) and above
   - **Rest:** Remove the roast from the oven and transfer it to a cutting board. Let it rest for 15-20 minutes before slicing.
2. **Make the Gravy:**
   - **Deglaze Pan:** While the roast rests, place the roasting pan on the stove over medium heat. Add beef broth to the pan, scraping up any browned bits from the bottom of the pan.
   - **Reduce Gravy:** Bring the mixture to a simmer and cook until slightly thickened. Adjust seasoning with salt and pepper if needed. Strain the gravy if desired and keep warm.

Yorkshire Pudding

Ingredients:

- 1 cup all-purpose flour
- 1 cup whole milk

- 3 large eggs
- 1/2 tsp salt
- 1/4 cup beef drippings or vegetable oil

Instructions:

1. **Prepare Batter:**
    - **Mix:** In a large bowl, whisk together flour, milk, eggs, and salt until smooth. Let the batter rest at room temperature for at least 30 minutes.
2. **Preheat Pan:**
    - **Heat Oil:** Place a 12-cup muffin tin or a large roasting pan in the oven and preheat to 450°F (230°C). Add a small amount of beef drippings or vegetable oil (about 1/2 tsp per cup) to each muffin cup or throughout the pan. Heat in the oven until the oil is very hot and shimmering.
3. **Bake Yorkshire Pudding:**
    - **Pour Batter:** Carefully remove the hot pan from the oven. Pour the rested batter evenly into each cup of the muffin tin or into the roasting pan, filling each about halfway.
    - **Bake:** Return the pan to the oven and bake for 20-25 minutes, or until the Yorkshire puddings have puffed up and are golden brown. Avoid opening the oven door during baking, as this can cause them to deflate.

Serve:

- **Slice and Serve:** Slice the roast beef and serve with the Yorkshire pudding. Ladle the gravy over the beef and Yorkshire puddings, and enjoy your classic Sunday roast dinner!

This meal pairs well with traditional sides like roasted vegetables, mashed potatoes, and a crisp green salad.

Chicken Satay

Ingredients:

For the Chicken Marinade:

- 1 lb (450 g) chicken breast or thighs, cut into bite-sized strips
- 2 tbsp soy sauce
- 1 tbsp fish sauce (optional, can substitute with additional soy sauce)
- 2 tbsp brown sugar
- 1 tbsp vegetable oil
- 2 cloves garlic, minced
- 1 tbsp fresh ginger, minced
- 1 tsp ground coriander
- 1 tsp ground cumin
- 1/2 tsp turmeric powder

For the Peanut Sauce:

- 1/2 cup creamy peanut butter
- 1/4 cup coconut milk
- 2 tbsp soy sauce
- 2 tbsp brown sugar
- 1 tbsp lime juice
- 1 clove garlic, minced
- 1/2 tsp grated ginger
- 1/4 tsp chili flakes or hot sauce (optional, for heat)
- Water, as needed to thin the sauce

For Serving:

- Skewers (wooden or metal)
- Fresh cilantro, chopped (for garnish)
- Lime wedges (for garnish)
- Cucumber slices (for garnish)
- Cooked jasmine rice or rice noodles

Instructions

1. **Marinate the Chicken:**
   - **Combine Marinade:** In a bowl, mix soy sauce, fish sauce (if using), brown sugar, vegetable oil, garlic, ginger, ground coriander, ground cumin, and turmeric powder.

- **Marinate Chicken:** Add chicken strips to the marinade and toss to coat. Cover and refrigerate for at least 30 minutes, or up to 2 hours for more flavor.

2. **Prepare the Peanut Sauce:**
   - **Mix Sauce Ingredients:** In a bowl, combine peanut butter, coconut milk, soy sauce, brown sugar, lime juice, minced garlic, grated ginger, and chili flakes or hot sauce (if using).
   - **Adjust Consistency:** Whisk until smooth. If the sauce is too thick, add water a little at a time until you reach your desired consistency. Set aside.

3. **Skewer and Grill the Chicken:**
   - **Prepare Skewers:** If using wooden skewers, soak them in water for 30 minutes to prevent burning.
   - **Skewer Chicken:** Thread the marinated chicken strips onto the skewers.
   - **Preheat Grill:** Preheat your grill to medium-high heat.
   - **Grill Chicken:** Place the skewers on the grill. Cook for about 3-4 minutes per side, or until the chicken is cooked through and has nice grill marks. The internal temperature should reach 165°F (74°C).

4. **Serve:**
   - **Plate:** Arrange the grilled chicken skewers on a serving platter. Drizzle with or serve alongside the peanut sauce.
   - **Garnish:** Garnish with fresh cilantro, lime wedges, and cucumber slices.
   - **Side:** Serve with jasmine rice or rice noodles.

Enjoy your Chicken Satay with its rich, flavorful peanut sauce!

Beef and Broccoli Stir-Fry

Ingredients

For the Beef Marinade:

- 1 lb (450 g) flank steak or sirloin, thinly sliced against the grain
- 2 tbsp soy sauce
- 1 tbsp cornstarch
- 1 tbsp rice wine or dry sherry (optional)
- 1 tbsp vegetable oil

For the Stir-Fry Sauce:

- 1/4 cup soy sauce
- 2 tbsp oyster sauce
- 1 tbsp hoisin sauce
- 1 tbsp brown sugar
- 1/2 cup beef broth (or water)
- 1 tsp sesame oil
- 1 tbsp cornstarch mixed with 1 tbsp water (for thickening)

For the Stir-Fry:

- 2 tbsp vegetable oil
- 2 cups broccoli florets
- 1 red bell pepper, sliced
- 1 cup snap peas or sugar snap peas
- 3 cloves garlic, minced
- 1 tbsp fresh ginger, minced
- Cooked rice or noodles, for serving
- Sesame seeds (optional, for garnish)
- Sliced green onions (optional, for garnish)

Instructions

1. **Marinate the Beef:**
    - **Combine Marinade:** In a bowl, mix soy sauce, cornstarch, rice wine or sherry (if using), and vegetable oil.
    - **Marinate Beef:** Add the sliced beef to the marinade, toss to coat, and let it marinate for at least 15 minutes or up to 1 hour in the refrigerator.
2. **Prepare the Stir-Fry Sauce:**

- **Mix Sauce Ingredients:** In a bowl, combine soy sauce, oyster sauce, hoisin sauce, brown sugar, beef broth, and sesame oil. Stir until the sugar is dissolved. Mix in the cornstarch-water mixture and set aside.

3. **Stir-Fry the Beef:**
    - **Heat Oil:** Heat 1 tbsp vegetable oil in a large skillet or wok over high heat.
    - **Cook Beef:** Add the marinated beef in a single layer and cook for 2-3 minutes per side, or until browned and cooked through. Remove the beef from the skillet and set aside.
4. **Stir-Fry the Vegetables:**
    - **Cook Vegetables:** In the same skillet or wok, add another 1 tbsp of vegetable oil. Add broccoli, bell pepper, and snap peas. Stir-fry for 3-4 minutes, or until vegetables are crisp-tender.
    - **Add Aromatics:** Add garlic and ginger and stir-fry for an additional 1 minute, until fragrant.
5. **Combine and Finish:**
    - **Return Beef:** Return the cooked beef to the skillet with the vegetables.
    - **Add Sauce:** Pour the stir-fry sauce over the beef and vegetables. Stir well to coat and cook for 2-3 minutes, or until the sauce has thickened and everything is heated through.
6. **Serve:**
    - **Plate:** Serve the beef and broccoli stir-fry over cooked rice or noodles.
    - **Garnish:** Garnish with sesame seeds and sliced green onions if desired.

Enjoy your Beef and Broccoli Stir-Fry! This dish is great for a quick weeknight dinner and pairs well with a side of steamed rice or noodles.

Lamb Shank Braised in Red Wine

Ingredients

For the Braise:

- 4 lamb shanks (about 1.5 lbs each)
- Salt and freshly ground black pepper
- 2 tbsp olive oil
- 1 large onion, finely chopped
- 2 carrots, peeled and chopped
- 2 celery stalks, chopped
- 4 cloves garlic, minced
- 1 cup red wine (such as Cabernet Sauvignon or Merlot)
- 2 cups beef or chicken broth
- 1 can (14.5 oz) diced tomatoes
- 2 tbsp tomato paste
- 1 tbsp fresh rosemary, chopped (or 1 tsp dried rosemary)
- 1 tbsp fresh thyme, chopped (or 1 tsp dried thyme)
- 2 bay leaves
- 1 tbsp balsamic vinegar (optional, for added depth)

For Serving:

- Mashed potatoes, polenta, or rice
- Fresh parsley, chopped (for garnish)

Instructions

1. **Preheat the Oven:**
   - Preheat your oven to 325°F (163°C).
2. **Prepare the Lamb Shanks:**
   - **Season:** Pat the lamb shanks dry with paper towels. Season generously with salt and pepper.
   - **Brown Lamb:** Heat olive oil in a large Dutch oven or heavy oven-safe pot over medium-high heat. Add the lamb shanks and brown on all sides, about 8-10 minutes. Remove the lamb shanks from the pot and set aside.
3. **Cook the Vegetables:**
   - **Sauté:** In the same pot, add onion, carrots, and celery. Cook, stirring occasionally, until the vegetables are softened, about 5 minutes.
   - **Add Garlic:** Stir in minced garlic and cook for another 1 minute until fragrant.
4. **Deglaze and Add Liquids:**

- **Deglaze:** Pour in the red wine, scraping up any browned bits from the bottom of the pot. Bring to a simmer and cook for about 5 minutes, allowing the wine to reduce slightly.
- **Add Broth and Tomatoes:** Stir in beef or chicken broth, diced tomatoes, and tomato paste. Add rosemary, thyme, and bay leaves. If using, add balsamic vinegar for extra depth.

5. **Braise the Lamb:**
   - **Return Lamb:** Return the browned lamb shanks to the pot, making sure they are mostly submerged in the liquid.
   - **Cover and Cook:** Cover the pot with a lid and transfer to the preheated oven. Braise for 2.5 to 3 hours, or until the lamb is very tender and easily falls off the bone.
6. **Finish and Serve:**
   - **Rest Lamb:** Remove the pot from the oven. Carefully transfer the lamb shanks to a plate and cover loosely with foil to keep warm.
   - **Reduce Sauce (Optional):** If you prefer a thicker sauce, place the pot on the stove over medium heat and simmer the liquid uncovered for about 10-15 minutes, until it has reduced and thickened slightly. Adjust seasoning with salt and pepper if needed.
   - **Serve:** Serve the lamb shanks over mashed potatoes, polenta, or rice. Spoon some of the braising liquid and vegetables over the top.
   - **Garnish:** Garnish with chopped fresh parsley.

Enjoy your Lamb Shank Braised in Red Wine! This dish is perfect for a special occasion or a comforting meal.

Veal Scaloppini

Ingredients

For the Veal:

- 1 lb (450 g) veal cutlets (scaloppini), pounded thin (about 1/4 inch thick)
- Salt and freshly ground black pepper
- 1/2 cup all-purpose flour, for dredging
- 2 tbsp olive oil
- 2 tbsp unsalted butter

For the Sauce:

- 1/2 cup dry white wine
- 1/2 cup chicken broth
- 2 tbsp fresh lemon juice (about 1 lemon)
- 2 tbsp capers, drained
- 2 cloves garlic, minced
- 1/4 cup chopped fresh parsley (optional, for garnish)

Instructions

1. **Prepare the Veal:**
   - **Season and Dredge:** Season the veal cutlets with salt and pepper. Lightly dredge each cutlet in flour, shaking off the excess.
2. **Cook the Veal:**
   - **Heat Oil and Butter:** In a large skillet, heat olive oil and butter over medium-high heat until the butter is melted and the mixture is hot.
   - **Sear Veal:** Add the veal cutlets to the skillet in a single layer. Cook for about 1-2 minutes per side, or until the veal is golden brown and cooked through. Remove the veal from the skillet and transfer to a plate. Cover loosely with foil to keep warm.
3. **Prepare the Sauce:**
   - **Sauté Garlic:** In the same skillet, add a little more oil if needed. Add the minced garlic and sauté for about 30 seconds, or until fragrant.
   - **Deglaze:** Pour in the white wine and bring to a simmer, scraping up any browned bits from the bottom of the pan.
   - **Add Broth and Lemon Juice:** Stir in the chicken broth and lemon juice. Simmer for 2-3 minutes, allowing the sauce to reduce slightly.
   - **Add Capers:** Stir in the capers and cook for an additional 1-2 minutes.
4. **Combine and Serve:**

- - **Return Veal:** Return the veal cutlets to the skillet and spoon the sauce over them. Cook for 1-2 minutes, until the veal is heated through and well coated with the sauce.
  - **Garnish (Optional):** Sprinkle with chopped fresh parsley if desired.
5. **Serve:**
   - **Plate:** Serve the veal scaloppini with the sauce spooned over the top. This dish pairs well with sides like sautéed spinach, mashed potatoes, or pasta.

Enjoy your Veal Scaloppini! This dish is perfect for a quick weeknight dinner or a special occasion.

Pork Carnitas

Ingredients

For the Pork Carnitas:

- 3-4 lbs (1.4-1.8 kg) pork shoulder (pork butt), trimmed and cut into 2-inch chunks
- 1 tbsp olive oil
- 1 large onion, coarsely chopped
- 4 cloves garlic, minced
- 1 orange, juiced (about 1/2 cup)
- 1 lime, juiced
- 1 cup chicken broth
- 2 tsp ground cumin
- 2 tsp dried oregano
- 1 tsp smoked paprika
- 1/2 tsp chili powder (optional, for heat)
- 2 bay leaves
- Salt and freshly ground black pepper, to taste

For Serving:

- Flour or corn tortillas
- Fresh cilantro, chopped
- Lime wedges
- Diced onions
- Salsa or pico de gallo
- Sliced radishes or pickled jalapeños (optional)

Instructions

1. **Prepare the Pork:**
   - **Season and Sear:** Season the pork chunks with salt and pepper. Heat olive oil in a large Dutch oven or heavy pot over medium-high heat. Add the pork chunks in batches and sear on all sides until browned. Transfer the seared pork to a plate.
2. **Cook the Aromatics:**
   - **Sauté Vegetables:** In the same pot, add chopped onion and cook for 3-4 minutes, until softened. Add minced garlic and cook for another 1 minute.
3. **Combine and Braise:**
   - **Add Ingredients:** Return the seared pork to the pot. Add orange juice, lime juice, chicken broth, ground cumin, dried oregano, smoked paprika, chili powder (if using), and bay leaves.

- **Simmer:** Bring to a boil, then reduce the heat to low. Cover and simmer for 2.5 to 3 hours, or until the pork is very tender and shreds easily with a fork.
4. **Shred the Pork:**
    - **Shred:** Remove the pork chunks from the pot and transfer to a cutting board. Use two forks to shred the meat into bite-sized pieces.
    - **Reduce Sauce:** Return the shredded pork to the pot. Simmer uncovered for an additional 10-15 minutes, or until the liquid is reduced and slightly thickened.
5. **Crisp the Pork (Optional):**
    - **Crisp Pork:** For crispy carnitas, preheat your oven to 425°F (220°C). Spread the shredded pork in a single layer on a baking sheet and roast for 15-20 minutes, or until the edges are crispy and caramelized. You can also crisp the pork in a hot skillet if preferred.
6. **Serve:**
    - **Assemble Tacos:** Serve the carnitas in warm tortillas. Top with fresh cilantro, diced onions, salsa or pico de gallo, and lime wedges. Add sliced radishes or pickled jalapeños if desired.

Enjoy your Pork Carnitas! This dish is perfect for taco nights, burrito bowls, or even as a topping for nachos.

Stuffed Cabbage Rolls

Ingredients

For the Cabbage Rolls:

- 1 large head of cabbage
- 1 lb (450 g) ground beef (or a mix of beef and pork)
- 1 cup cooked rice (white or brown)
- 1 small onion, finely chopped
- 2 cloves garlic, minced
- 1 egg
- 1/2 cup fresh parsley, chopped
- 1 tsp dried thyme
- Salt and freshly ground black pepper, to taste

For the Sauce:

- 1 can (15 oz) tomato sauce
- 1 can (15 oz) diced tomatoes
- 2 tbsp brown sugar
- 2 tbsp lemon juice (about 1 lemon)
- 1 tsp paprika
- 1/2 tsp dried oregano
- Salt and freshly ground black pepper, to taste

Instructions

1. **Prepare the Cabbage:**
   - **Cook Cabbage:** Bring a large pot of water to a boil. Carefully remove the core from the cabbage and place the head into the boiling water. Cook for 2-3 minutes or until the outer leaves are pliable. Remove the cabbage and let it cool slightly.
   - **Peel Leaves:** Gently peel off the large outer leaves. Set aside and pat dry. You'll need about 12-15 leaves, depending on their size.
2. **Prepare the Filling:**
   - **Combine Ingredients:** In a large bowl, mix together the ground beef, cooked rice, chopped onion, minced garlic, egg, parsley, thyme, salt, and pepper until well combined.
3. **Assemble the Rolls:**
   - **Fill Cabbage Leaves:** Place a generous spoonful of the meat mixture onto the center of each cabbage leaf. Fold in the sides and roll up the leaf to enclose the filling. Secure with toothpicks if needed.
   - **Repeat:** Continue until all the filling is used.

4. **Prepare the Sauce:**
   - **Mix Sauce Ingredients:** In a bowl, combine tomato sauce, diced tomatoes, brown sugar, lemon juice, paprika, oregano, salt, and pepper. Stir well.
5. **Cook the Cabbage Rolls:**
   - **Layer Rolls:** Spread a small amount of the sauce on the bottom of a large baking dish or Dutch oven. Arrange the cabbage rolls seam side down in a single layer. Pour the remaining sauce over the rolls.
   - **Cover and Bake:** Cover with foil or a lid. Bake in a preheated oven at 350°F (175°C) for 1.5 to 2 hours, or until the cabbage is tender and the filling is cooked through.
6. **Serve:**
   - **Rest:** Let the cabbage rolls rest for a few minutes before serving. Remove toothpicks if used.
   - **Garnish:** Serve with additional chopped parsley if desired.

Enjoy your Stuffed Cabbage Rolls! This dish is perfect for a hearty family meal and pairs well with a side of crusty bread or a fresh salad.

Chicken Kiev

Ingredients

For the Garlic Herb Butter:

- 1/2 cup (1 stick) unsalted butter, softened
- 3 cloves garlic, minced
- 2 tbsp fresh parsley, chopped
- 1 tbsp fresh dill, chopped (or 1 tsp dried dill)
- 1 tbsp fresh chives, chopped
- 1 tsp lemon juice
- Salt and freshly ground black pepper, to taste

For the Chicken:

- 4 boneless, skinless chicken breasts
- Salt and freshly ground black pepper, to taste
- 1/2 cup all-purpose flour
- 2 large eggs
- 1 cup bread crumbs (plain or panko)
- 1/2 cup grated Parmesan cheese (optional, for added flavor)
- Vegetable oil, for frying (optional)

Instructions

1. **Prepare the Garlic Herb Butter:**
   - **Mix Ingredients:** In a bowl, combine the softened butter, minced garlic, chopped parsley, dill, chives, lemon juice, salt, and pepper. Mix until well combined.
   - **Shape Butter:** Place the butter mixture onto a piece of plastic wrap. Roll into a log shape and freeze until firm, about 30 minutes.
2. **Prepare the Chicken:**
   - **Pound Chicken:** Place each chicken breast between two sheets of plastic wrap or parchment paper. Use a meat mallet or rolling pin to pound the chicken to an even thickness, about 1/2 inch thick.
   - **Season:** Season the chicken breasts with salt and pepper.
3. **Stuff the Chicken:**
   - **Cut Butter:** Once the garlic herb butter is firm, slice it into 4 equal portions.
   - **Fill Chicken:** Place a portion of the butter in the center of each chicken breast. Fold in the sides of the chicken and roll it up, securing with toothpicks or tying with kitchen twine if necessary.
4. **Bread the Chicken:**

- **Prepare Breading Station:** Set up a breading station with three shallow dishes: one with flour, one with beaten eggs, and one with bread crumbs mixed with Parmesan cheese (if using).
- **Bread Chicken:** Dredge each stuffed chicken breast in flour, shaking off the excess. Dip into the beaten eggs, then coat with the bread crumb mixture, pressing gently to adhere.

5. **Cook the Chicken:**
   - **Preheat Oven:** Preheat your oven to 375°F (190°C).
   - **Pan-Fry (Optional):** For a crispier crust, heat vegetable oil in a large skillet over medium-high heat. Add the breaded chicken breasts and cook for 2-3 minutes per side, or until golden brown. Remove from the skillet and transfer to a baking dish.
   - **Bake:** If not pan-frying, place the breaded chicken breasts directly on a baking sheet or in a baking dish. Bake in the preheated oven for 20-25 minutes, or until the chicken is cooked through and the internal temperature reaches 165°F (74°C).
6. **Serve:**
   - **Rest:** Let the chicken rest for a few minutes before removing toothpicks or twine.
   - **Garnish:** Serve with a garnish of fresh herbs if desired.

Enjoy your Chicken Kiev! This dish is delicious served with mashed potatoes, steamed vegetables, or a crisp green salad.

Beef Empanadas

Ingredients

For the Dough:

- 2 1/2 cups all-purpose flour
- 1/2 cup unsalted butter, cold and cubed
- 1/2 tsp salt
- 1 large egg
- 1/4 cup cold water (more if needed)

For the Beef Filling:

- 1 lb (450 g) ground beef
- 1 medium onion, finely chopped
- 1 red bell pepper, finely chopped
- 2 cloves garlic, minced
- 1/2 cup green olives, pitted and chopped (optional)
- 1/2 cup raisins (optional)
- 1 tsp ground cumin
- 1 tsp paprika
- 1/2 tsp dried oregano
- Salt and freshly ground black pepper, to taste
- 1/2 cup beef broth
- 1 large egg, beaten (for egg wash)

Instructions

1. **Prepare the Dough:**
    - **Mix Dry Ingredients:** In a large bowl, whisk together the flour and salt.
    - **Cut in Butter:** Add the cold, cubed butter to the flour. Use a pastry cutter or your fingers to cut the butter into the flour until the mixture resembles coarse crumbs.
    - **Add Egg and Water:** Beat the egg and mix it into the flour mixture. Gradually add cold water, one tablespoon at a time, until the dough just comes together. You may need a little more or less water.
    - **Chill Dough:** Turn the dough out onto a lightly floured surface and knead a few times until smooth. Wrap in plastic wrap and refrigerate for at least 30 minutes.
2. **Prepare the Beef Filling:**
    - **Cook Beef:** Heat a large skillet over medium heat. Add the ground beef and cook until browned, breaking it up with a spoon.
    - **Add Vegetables:** Add the chopped onion, red bell pepper, and garlic. Cook until the vegetables are softened, about 5 minutes.

- **Season and Simmer:** Stir in the cumin, paprika, oregano, salt, and pepper. If using, add olives and raisins. Pour in the beef broth and cook until the mixture is thickened and most of the liquid has evaporated. Let the filling cool slightly.

3. **Assemble the Empanadas:**
   - **Preheat Oven:** Preheat your oven to 375°F (190°C).
   - **Roll Out Dough:** On a lightly floured surface, roll out the chilled dough to about 1/8 inch thickness. Use a round cutter (about 4-5 inches in diameter) to cut out circles.
   - **Fill and Seal:** Place a spoonful of the beef filling in the center of each dough circle. Fold the dough over to create a half-moon shape. Use a fork to press the edges together and seal them. You can also crimp the edges with your fingers for a decorative touch.
   - **Egg Wash:** Place the empanadas on a baking sheet lined with parchment paper. Brush the tops with the beaten egg.

4. **Bake:**
   - **Bake Empanadas:** Bake in the preheated oven for 20-25 minutes, or until the empanadas are golden brown and crisp.

5. **Serve:**
   - **Cool Slightly:** Let the empanadas cool for a few minutes before serving.
   - **Garnish:** Serve warm or at room temperature. They are great on their own or with a dipping sauce like salsa or chimichurri.

Enjoy your Beef Empanadas! They make a fantastic appetizer or a hearty snack.

BBQ Chicken

Ingredients

For the Chicken:

- 4 bone-in, skin-on chicken thighs (or breasts, drumsticks, or a mix)
- Salt and freshly ground black pepper, to taste
- 1 tbsp olive oil (for grilling or baking)

For the BBQ Sauce:

- 1 cup ketchup
- 1/2 cup brown sugar
- 1/4 cup apple cider vinegar
- 1/4 cup honey
- 2 tbsp Worcestershire sauce
- 1 tbsp smoked paprika
- 1 tbsp Dijon mustard
- 1 tsp garlic powder
- 1 tsp onion powder
- 1/2 tsp cayenne pepper (optional, for heat)
- Salt and freshly ground black pepper, to taste

Instructions

1. **Prepare the BBQ Sauce:**
   - **Combine Ingredients:** In a medium saucepan, combine ketchup, brown sugar, apple cider vinegar, honey, Worcestershire sauce, smoked paprika, Dijon mustard, garlic powder, onion powder, and cayenne pepper (if using).
   - **Simmer:** Bring to a simmer over medium heat. Reduce the heat to low and cook for about 10-15 minutes, stirring occasionally, until the sauce is thickened and flavors are well combined. Season with salt and pepper to taste. Set aside to cool.
2. **Prepare the Chicken:**
   - **Season:** Pat the chicken pieces dry with paper towels. Season generously with salt and pepper.
   - **Preheat Oven/Grill:** Preheat your grill to medium heat (about 350°F/175°C) or your oven to 375°F (190°C).
3. **Cook the Chicken:**
   For Grilling:
   - **Oil the Grill:** Brush the grill grates with oil to prevent sticking.

- **Grill Chicken:** Place the chicken pieces on the grill and cook for about 25-30 minutes, turning occasionally, until the chicken reaches an internal temperature of 165°F (74°C) and has a nice char. Baste with BBQ sauce during the last 10 minutes of grilling.
4. **For Baking:**
    - **Prepare Baking Sheet:** Brush a baking sheet with olive oil or line it with parchment paper.
    - **Bake Chicken:** Place the chicken pieces on the prepared baking sheet. Bake for 30-35 minutes, or until the chicken reaches an internal temperature of 165°F (74°C). During the last 10 minutes of baking, brush with BBQ sauce and return to the oven to caramelize.
5. **Serve:**
    - **Rest Chicken:** Allow the chicken to rest for a few minutes before serving.
    - **Garnish:** Serve with additional BBQ sauce on the side. Garnish with chopped fresh parsley or cilantro if desired.
6. **Optional Sides:**
    - **Serve With:** BBQ chicken pairs wonderfully with classic sides like coleslaw, baked beans, corn on the cob, or a fresh green salad.

Enjoy your BBQ Chicken! Whether you're cooking it on the grill or in the oven, this recipe is sure to be a hit at your next meal.

Slow Cooker Beef Chili

Ingredients

For the Chili:

- 2 lbs (900 g) ground beef
- 1 large onion, chopped
- 4 cloves garlic, minced
- 1 red bell pepper, chopped
- 1 green bell pepper, chopped
- 2 (14.5 oz) cans diced tomatoes
- 1 (15 oz) can kidney beans, drained and rinsed
- 1 (15 oz) can black beans, drained and rinsed
- 1 cup beef broth
- 1/4 cup tomato paste
- 2 tbsp chili powder
- 1 tsp ground cumin
- 1 tsp smoked paprika
- 1/2 tsp dried oregano
- 1/2 tsp ground cayenne pepper (optional, for heat)
- Salt and freshly ground black pepper, to taste

For Serving:

- Shredded cheese (cheddar or Monterey Jack)
- Sour cream
- Chopped fresh cilantro
- Sliced green onions
- Crushed tortilla chips or cornbread

Instructions

1. **Prepare the Ingredients:**
   - **Brown the Beef:** In a large skillet over medium-high heat, cook the ground beef until browned. Break it up into small pieces as it cooks. Drain excess fat if necessary.
   - **Cook Vegetables:** Add the chopped onion, garlic, and bell peppers to the skillet with the beef. Cook for about 5 minutes, or until the vegetables are softened.
2. **Transfer to Slow Cooker:**
   - **Combine Ingredients:** Transfer the cooked beef and vegetables to the slow cooker.

- **Add Remaining Ingredients:** Add diced tomatoes, kidney beans, black beans, beef broth, tomato paste, chili powder, cumin, smoked paprika, oregano, cayenne pepper (if using), salt, and pepper to the slow cooker. Stir well to combine.

3. **Cook:**
   - **Set Slow Cooker:** Cover and cook on low for 6-8 hours or on high for 3-4 hours, until the chili is thickened and the flavors are well melded.
4. **Finish and Serve:**
   - **Adjust Seasoning:** Taste and adjust seasoning with additional salt and pepper if needed.
   - **Serve:** Ladle the chili into bowls and top with shredded cheese, sour cream, chopped cilantro, and sliced green onions. Serve with crushed tortilla chips or cornbread on the side.

Tips

- **For a thicker chili:** Mash some of the beans with a spoon or fork, or stir in a bit of cornstarch mixed with water during the last 30 minutes of cooking.
- **For extra flavor:** You can sauté additional spices like cumin or smoked paprika before adding them to the slow cooker to enhance their flavor.

Enjoy your Slow Cooker Beef Chili! It's a satisfying and delicious meal that's perfect for cozy nights or feeding a crowd.

Grilled Lamb Kebabs

Ingredients

For the Marinade:

- 1/2 cup plain Greek yogurt
- 2 tbsp olive oil
- 2 tbsp lemon juice (about 1 lemon)
- 3 cloves garlic, minced
- 2 tbsp fresh rosemary, chopped (or 1 tbsp dried rosemary)
- 2 tbsp fresh thyme, chopped (or 1 tbsp dried thyme)
- 1 tsp ground cumin
- 1 tsp smoked paprika
- 1/2 tsp ground coriander
- 1/2 tsp cayenne pepper (optional, for heat)
- Salt and freshly ground black pepper, to taste

For the Lamb Kebabs:

- 1 1/2 lbs (680 g) lamb shoulder or leg, trimmed and cut into 1-inch cubes
- 1 red onion, cut into wedges
- 1 red bell pepper, cut into chunks
- 1 green bell pepper, cut into chunks
- 1 zucchini, sliced into rounds (optional)
- Wooden or metal skewers (if using wooden skewers, soak them in water for at least 30 minutes to prevent burning)

Instructions

1. **Prepare the Marinade:**
    - **Combine Ingredients:** In a large bowl, whisk together Greek yogurt, olive oil, lemon juice, minced garlic, rosemary, thyme, cumin, smoked paprika, ground coriander, cayenne pepper (if using), salt, and pepper.
2. **Marinate the Lamb:**
    - **Marinate:** Add the lamb cubes to the bowl with the marinade. Toss well to coat. Cover and refrigerate for at least 2 hours or overnight for the best flavor.
3. **Prepare the Vegetables:**
    - **Cut and Season:** If using vegetables, cut them into chunks similar in size to the lamb. You can season them with a bit of olive oil, salt, and pepper if desired.
4. **Assemble the Kebabs:**
    - **Skewer Ingredients:** Thread the marinated lamb cubes onto skewers, alternating with pieces of red onion, bell peppers, and zucchini (if using). Leave a bit of space between each piece to ensure even cooking.
5. **Grill the Kebabs:**

        - **Preheat Grill:** Preheat your grill to medium-high heat.
        - **Grill Lamb:** Place the skewers on the grill. Cook for 10-15 minutes, turning occasionally, until the lamb reaches your desired level of doneness (145°F/63°C for medium-rare, 160°F/71°C for medium).
        - **Check Vegetables:** If using vegetables, make sure they are tender and have nice grill marks.
6. **Serve:**
        - **Rest Lamb:** Allow the kebabs to rest for a few minutes before serving.
        - **Garnish:** Serve the kebabs with your favorite sides such as couscous, rice, or a fresh salad. You can also serve with a side of tzatziki sauce or a squeeze of fresh lemon juice.

Tips

- **For Extra Flavor:** Try adding a splash of balsamic vinegar or a teaspoon of ground cinnamon to the marinade for additional depth.
- **Avoid Overcrowding:** Don't overcrowd the skewers; give each piece enough space for even grilling.

Enjoy your Grilled Lamb Kebabs! They're perfect for a casual barbecue or a special dinner.

Shepherd's Pie

Ingredients

For the Meat Filling:

- 1 lb (450 g) ground beef or lamb (for traditional Shepherd's Pie, use lamb; for Cottage Pie, use beef)
- 1 medium onion, finely chopped
- 2 cloves garlic, minced
- 2 carrots, peeled and diced
- 1 cup frozen peas
- 1 cup beef or vegetable broth
- 2 tbsp tomato paste
- 1 tbsp Worcestershire sauce
- 1 tsp dried thyme
- 1/2 tsp dried rosemary
- Salt and freshly ground black pepper, to taste
- 2 tbsp olive oil or butter (for cooking)

For the Mashed Potatoes:

- 2 lbs (900 g) potatoes (russet or Yukon Gold), peeled and cubed
- 1/2 cup milk
- 1/4 cup unsalted butter
- Salt and freshly ground black pepper, to taste

Instructions

1. **Prepare the Mashed Potatoes:**
    - **Cook Potatoes:** Place the peeled and cubed potatoes in a large pot of salted water. Bring to a boil and cook until tender, about 15-20 minutes.
    - **Mash:** Drain the potatoes and return them to the pot. Add milk and butter. Mash until smooth and creamy. Season with salt and pepper to taste. Set aside.
2. **Prepare the Meat Filling:**
    - **Cook Meat:** Heat olive oil or butter in a large skillet over medium heat. Add the ground beef or lamb and cook until browned. Drain any excess fat.
    - **Add Vegetables:** Add the chopped onion, garlic, and diced carrots to the skillet. Cook for about 5 minutes, until the vegetables are softened.
    - **Add Flavorings:** Stir in the tomato paste, Worcestershire sauce, thyme, and rosemary. Cook for another minute.
    - **Simmer:** Add the broth and bring the mixture to a simmer. Cook for about 10 minutes, or until the liquid has reduced and the filling is thickened. Stir in the frozen peas and cook for an additional 2 minutes. Season with salt and pepper to taste.
3. **Assemble the Shepherd's Pie:**
    - **Preheat Oven:** Preheat your oven to 375°F (190°C).

- **Layer:** Transfer the meat filling to a baking dish and spread it out evenly. Spoon the mashed potatoes over the meat filling, spreading them out with a spatula. You can use a fork to create texture on top of the mashed potatoes for a more rustic look.
4. **Bake:**
    - **Bake Pie:** Bake in the preheated oven for 20-25 minutes, or until the top is golden brown and the filling is bubbling around the edges.
5. **Serve:**
    - **Rest and Serve:** Allow the Shepherd's Pie to cool for a few minutes before serving. This helps it set and makes it easier to portion.

Tips

- **For Extra Flavor:** You can mix some grated cheese into the mashed potatoes or sprinkle it on top before baking for a cheesy crust.
- **Add Greens:** Feel free to add other vegetables to the meat filling, such as corn or mushrooms, to suit your taste.

Enjoy your Shepherd's Pie! This dish is a comforting and hearty meal that's perfect for any time of year.

Teriyaki Beef Skewers

Ingredients

For the Teriyaki Marinade:

- 1/2 cup soy sauce
- 1/4 cup mirin (sweet rice wine) or white wine
- 1/4 cup brown sugar
- 2 tbsp honey
- 2 tbsp rice vinegar
- 2 cloves garlic, minced
- 1 tbsp fresh ginger, grated (or 1 tsp ground ginger)
- 1 tsp sesame oil
- 1 tbsp cornstarch (optional, for thickening)

For the Beef Skewers:

- 1 1/2 lbs (680 g) sirloin steak or flank steak, cut into 1-inch cubes
- 1 red bell pepper, cut into chunks
- 1 green bell pepper, cut into chunks
- 1 red onion, cut into wedges
- 1 cup cherry tomatoes (optional)
- Wooden or metal skewers (if using wooden skewers, soak them in water for at least 30 minutes to prevent burning)

Instructions

1. **Prepare the Marinade:**
    - **Combine Ingredients:** In a medium bowl, whisk together soy sauce, mirin, brown sugar, honey, rice vinegar, minced garlic, grated ginger, and sesame oil. If you prefer a thicker marinade, dissolve the cornstarch in 2 tablespoons of water and stir it into the marinade.
2. **Marinate the Beef:**
    - **Marinate:** Place the cubed beef in a resealable plastic bag or a shallow dish. Pour half of the teriyaki marinade over the beef. Seal the bag or cover the dish and refrigerate for at least 1 hour, or up to 8 hours for more flavor. Reserve the remaining marinade for basting and serving.
3. **Prepare the Skewers:**
    - **Assemble:** Thread the marinated beef onto the skewers, alternating with chunks of bell peppers, onion, and cherry tomatoes (if using). Leave a bit of space between each piece to ensure even cooking.
4. **Grill the Skewers:**
    - **Preheat Grill:** Preheat your grill to medium-high heat.
    - **Grill:** Place the skewers on the grill and cook for about 10-15 minutes, turning occasionally, until the beef is cooked to your desired level of doneness. Baste with the reserved marinade during the last few minutes of grilling.

5. **Serve:**
    - **Rest and Garnish:** Allow the skewers to rest for a few minutes before serving. Garnish with sesame seeds or chopped green onions if desired.
    - **Serve With:** Serve the teriyaki beef skewers over steamed rice, with a side of grilled vegetables, or a fresh salad.

Tips

- **Thickening Marinade:** If you want to use the marinade as a sauce, you can simmer it in a saucepan until it thickens slightly. Make sure to bring it to a boil to ensure it is safe to consume, as it has been in contact with raw meat.
- **Alternate Cooking Method:** If you don't have access to a grill, you can broil the skewers in the oven. Place them on a broiler pan and cook under the broiler for about 10 minutes, turning once.

Enjoy your Teriyaki Beef Skewers! They are a delicious and versatile dish that's great for summer barbecues or a quick and tasty dinner.

Peking Duck

Ingredients

For the Duck:

- 1 whole duck (about 5-6 lbs), thawed if frozen
- 2 tbsp maltose or honey (for glazing)
- 2 tbsp soy sauce
- 1 tbsp rice vinegar
- 1 tbsp hoisin sauce
- 1 tbsp Chinese five-spice powder
- 1 tbsp salt
- 1/2 tsp ground white pepper

For Serving:

- Mandarin pancakes or thin flour tortillas
- Hoisin sauce
- Thinly sliced cucumber
- Thinly sliced green onions

Instructions

1. **Prepare the Duck:**
    - **Clean the Duck:** Remove any excess fat from the duck and pat it dry with paper towels. Trim the neck and giblets if still attached. You can save these for making broth if desired.
    - **Season the Duck:** Rub the duck inside and out with salt and white pepper. Sprinkle the Chinese five-spice powder inside the cavity.
2. **Prepare the Glaze:**
    - **Combine Ingredients:** In a small bowl, mix together maltose or honey, soy sauce, rice vinegar, and hoisin sauce until well combined. If the maltose is too thick, you can gently warm it to make it easier to mix.
3. **Dry the Duck:**
    - **Air-Dry:** Place the duck on a rack over a baking sheet or tray. Brush the duck with the glaze mixture, making sure to coat it evenly. Allow the duck to air-dry in the refrigerator, uncovered, for at least 6 hours, or overnight for best results. This helps the skin become crispy.
4. **Roast the Duck:**
    - **Preheat Oven:** Preheat your oven to 375°F (190°C).
    - **Prepare for Roasting:** Place the duck on a rack in a roasting pan. If you don't have a rack, you can place the duck directly in the pan, but a rack helps the fat drain away from the duck.
    - **Roast:** Roast the duck in the preheated oven for about 1.5 to 2 hours, or until the skin is golden brown and crispy. Baste the duck occasionally with the pan juices or additional glaze, if desired.

5. **Crisp the Skin (Optional):**
   - **Broil:** If the skin isn't as crispy as you'd like, you can finish the duck under the broiler for a few minutes, watching carefully to avoid burning.
6. **Rest and Carve:**
   - **Rest Duck:** Let the duck rest for about 15 minutes before carving.
   - **Carve:** Carve the duck into thin slices, focusing on getting pieces of crispy skin and meat.
7. **Serve:**
   - **Prepare Pancakes:** Warm the Mandarin pancakes or tortillas according to package instructions.
   - **Serve:** Serve the duck slices with hoisin sauce, thinly sliced cucumber, and green onions. Place the duck, sauce, cucumber, and onions on the table and let diners assemble their own pancakes or tortillas.

Tips

- **For Extra Crispiness:** You can use a fan or a hairdryer (on a cool setting) to blow air over the duck skin while it's drying in the refrigerator. This can help achieve even crispier skin.
- **Saving the Fat:** The rendered duck fat is excellent for roasting vegetables or making other dishes. Strain and store it in a jar in the refrigerator.

Enjoy your homemade Peking Duck! It's a delightful and elegant dish that's sure to impress.

Beef Tenderloin with Horseradish Sauce

Ingredients

For the Beef Tenderloin:

- 2 lbs (900 g) beef tenderloin, trimmed
- 2 tbsp olive oil
- 2 tbsp fresh rosemary, chopped (or 1 tbsp dried rosemary)
- 2 tbsp fresh thyme, chopped (or 1 tbsp dried thyme)
- 2 cloves garlic, minced
- Salt and freshly ground black pepper, to taste

For the Horseradish Sauce:

- 1/2 cup sour cream
- 2 tbsp prepared horseradish (adjust to taste)
- 1 tbsp Dijon mustard
- 1 tbsp lemon juice
- 1 tbsp fresh chives, chopped (optional)
- Salt and freshly ground black pepper, to taste

Instructions

1. **Prepare the Beef Tenderloin:**
    - **Preheat Oven:** Preheat your oven to 400°F (200°C).
    - **Season the Beef:** Pat the beef tenderloin dry with paper towels. Rub it all over with olive oil. Season generously with salt, pepper, minced garlic, rosemary, and thyme.
    - **Sear the Beef:** Heat a large ovenproof skillet over medium-high heat. Add the beef tenderloin and sear on all sides until browned, about 3-4 minutes per side.
2. **Roast the Beef:**
    - **Roast in Oven:** Transfer the skillet to the preheated oven. Roast for about 20-25 minutes, or until the internal temperature reaches 125°F (52°C) for medium-rare or 135°F (57°C) for medium. Use a meat thermometer for accurate results.
    - **Rest the Meat:** Remove the beef from the oven and transfer it to a cutting board. Cover loosely with foil and let it rest for 10-15 minutes before slicing. This helps the juices redistribute and makes for a more tender roast.
3. **Prepare the Horseradish Sauce:**
    - **Combine Ingredients:** In a small bowl, mix together sour cream, prepared horseradish, Dijon mustard, lemon juice, and chopped chives (if using). Season with salt and pepper to taste. Adjust the horseradish to your preference for spiciness.
4. **Serve:**
    - **Slice the Beef:** Slice the rested beef tenderloin into 1/2-inch to 1-inch thick slices.
    - **Serve with Sauce:** Arrange the slices on a serving platter or individual plates. Serve with the horseradish sauce on the side.

Tips

- **For Extra Flavor:** You can marinate the beef tenderloin in the herb and garlic mixture for a few hours or overnight for a more intense flavor.
- **Beef Tenderloin Doneness:** Keep in mind that the beef will continue to cook slightly as it rests, so aim for a temperature a few degrees below your desired doneness.

Enjoy your Beef Tenderloin with Horseradish Sauce! It's a classic dish that's sure to impress your guests with its rich flavors and elegant presentation.

Chicken and Sausage Gumbo

Ingredients

For the Gumbo:

- 1/2 cup vegetable oil
- 1/2 cup all-purpose flour
- 1 large onion, chopped
- 1 bell pepper (red or green), chopped
- 3 celery stalks, chopped
- 4 cloves garlic, minced
- 1 lb (450 g) chicken thighs, boneless and skinless, cut into bite-sized pieces
- 12 oz (340 g) andouille sausage or smoked sausage, sliced into rounds
- 1 (14.5 oz) can diced tomatoes
- 4 cups chicken broth
- 2 bay leaves
- 1 tbsp Creole seasoning (or to taste)
- 1 tsp dried thyme
- 1/2 tsp paprika
- 1/2 tsp cayenne pepper (adjust to taste)
- 1 cup okra, sliced (fresh or frozen)
- 2 cups cooked white rice (for serving)
- Chopped fresh parsley (for garnish)
- Chopped green onions (for garnish)

Instructions

1. **Make the Roux:**
    - **Combine Ingredients:** In a large pot or Dutch oven, heat the vegetable oil over medium heat. Gradually whisk in the flour to create a roux.
    - **Cook the Roux:** Cook the roux, stirring constantly, until it turns a dark brown color (about the color of chocolate) and has a nutty aroma, approximately 15-20 minutes. Be careful not to burn it.
2. **Prepare the Vegetables:**
    - **Add Vegetables:** Add the chopped onion, bell pepper, celery, and garlic to the roux. Cook, stirring occasionally, until the vegetables are softened, about 5 minutes.
3. **Cook the Meat:**
    - **Add Chicken and Sausage:** Add the chicken pieces and sausage to the pot. Cook for about 5 minutes, stirring occasionally, until the chicken starts to brown.
4. **Add Liquids and Seasonings:**
    - **Add Tomatoes and Broth:** Stir in the diced tomatoes, chicken broth, bay leaves, Creole seasoning, dried thyme, paprika, and cayenne pepper. Bring to a boil, then reduce the heat to low.
    - **Simmer:** Cover and simmer for about 30 minutes, or until the chicken is cooked through and tender.
5. **Add Okra:**

- **Incorporate Okra:** Stir in the sliced okra. Continue to simmer uncovered for an additional 10-15 minutes, until the okra is tender and the gumbo has thickened.
6. **Serve:**
    - **Prepare Rice:** Spoon cooked rice into bowls or into the center of a serving platter.
    - **Serve Gumbo:** Ladle the gumbo over the rice.
    - **Garnish:** Garnish with chopped parsley and green onions.

Tips

- **For a Thicker Gumbo:** If you prefer a thicker gumbo, you can simmer it longer to reduce the liquid or stir in a slurry of cornstarch and water during the last few minutes of cooking.
- **Adjust Spice Levels:** Adjust the amount of cayenne pepper and Creole seasoning to suit your spice preference.

Enjoy your Chicken and Sausage Gumbo! It's a hearty and flavorful dish that captures the essence of Southern cooking.

Beef and Mushroom Pie

Ingredients

For the Filling:

- 1 lb (450 g) beef stew meat, cut into bite-sized pieces
- 2 tbsp olive oil
- 1 large onion, chopped
- 2 cloves garlic, minced
- 8 oz (225 g) mushrooms, sliced (button or cremini)
- 1/4 cup all-purpose flour
- 1 cup beef broth
- 1/2 cup red wine (optional, replace with more beef broth if preferred)
- 2 tbsp tomato paste
- 1 tbsp Worcestershire sauce
- 1 tsp dried thyme
- 1/2 tsp dried rosemary
- Salt and freshly ground black pepper, to taste
- 1 cup frozen peas (optional, for added color and texture)

For the Pie:

- 1 package (about 14 oz) of store-bought or homemade pie crusts (enough for top and bottom)
- 1 egg, beaten (for egg wash)
- Fresh herbs for garnish (optional)

Instructions

1. **Prepare the Filling:**
    - **Brown the Beef:** Heat olive oil in a large skillet or Dutch oven over medium-high heat. Add the beef pieces and cook until browned on all sides. Remove the beef from the skillet and set aside.
    - **Cook Vegetables:** In the same skillet, add the chopped onion and cook until softened, about 5 minutes. Add the minced garlic and sliced mushrooms and cook until the mushrooms are browned and any liquid has evaporated, about 5 minutes.
    - **Thicken the Filling:** Sprinkle the flour over the vegetables and stir to coat. Cook for another 2 minutes to eliminate the raw flour taste.
    - **Add Liquids and Simmer:** Gradually stir in the beef broth and red wine, scraping up any browned bits from the bottom of the pan. Stir in the tomato paste, Worcestershire sauce, thyme, rosemary, salt, and pepper. Return the beef to the skillet.
    - **Simmer:** Bring to a simmer, cover, and cook on low heat for about 45 minutes, or until the beef is tender and the gravy has thickened. Stir in the frozen peas if using.
2. **Prepare the Pie:**
    - **Preheat Oven:** Preheat your oven to 400°F (200°C).

- **Prepare Pie Crust:** Roll out the bottom pie crust and fit it into a 9-inch pie dish. Trim any excess overhanging edges.
- **Fill the Pie:** Pour the beef and mushroom filling into the pie crust.
- **Add Top Crust:** Roll out the top pie crust and place it over the filling. Trim and crimp the edges to seal. Cut a few slits in the top crust to allow steam to escape.
- **Brush with Egg Wash:** Brush the top crust with the beaten egg for a golden finish.

3. **Bake the Pie:**
   - **Bake:** Place the pie on a baking sheet (to catch any drips) and bake in the preheated oven for 30-35 minutes, or until the crust is golden brown and the filling is bubbling.
   - **Cool:** Allow the pie to cool for 10-15 minutes before serving to let the filling set.
4. **Serve:**
   - **Garnish (Optional):** Garnish with fresh herbs if desired.
   - **Enjoy:** Serve warm with a side of vegetables or a simple salad.

Tips

- **For a Crispier Bottom Crust:** Pre-bake the bottom crust for 10 minutes before adding the filling to prevent it from getting soggy.
- **Homemade Crust:** If you prefer homemade pie crust, use your favorite recipe or one from scratch.

Enjoy your Beef and Mushroom Pie! It's a classic and comforting dish that's sure to please.

Chicken Piccata

Ingredients

For the Chicken:

- 4 boneless, skinless chicken breasts
- 1/2 cup all-purpose flour
- Salt and freshly ground black pepper, to taste
- 1/4 cup olive oil
- 2 tbsp unsalted butter

For the Sauce:

- 1/2 cup chicken broth
- 1/2 cup dry white wine (optional; replace with more chicken broth if preferred)
- Juice of 1 lemon
- 1/4 cup capers, drained and rinsed
- 2 cloves garlic, minced
- 1 tbsp fresh parsley, chopped (for garnish)
- Lemon slices (for garnish, optional)

Instructions

1. **Prepare the Chicken:**
   - **Pound the Chicken:** Place the chicken breasts between two sheets of plastic wrap or parchment paper. Use a meat mallet or rolling pin to gently pound the chicken to an even thickness, about 1/2 inch thick. This helps the chicken cook evenly.
   - **Season and Dredge:** Season both sides of the chicken breasts with salt and pepper. Dredge each breast in the flour, shaking off any excess.
2. **Cook the Chicken:**
   - **Heat Oil and Butter:** In a large skillet, heat the olive oil and 1 tablespoon of butter over medium-high heat.
   - **Sear the Chicken:** Add the chicken breasts to the skillet and cook for about 4-5 minutes on each side, or until the chicken is golden brown and cooked through (internal temperature should reach 165°F/74°C). Transfer the chicken to a plate and cover with foil to keep warm.
3. **Prepare the Sauce:**
   - **Deglaze the Pan:** In the same skillet, add a bit more oil if needed and sauté the minced garlic for about 30 seconds until fragrant. Pour in the white wine (if using) and chicken broth, scraping up any browned bits from the bottom of the pan. Bring to a simmer and cook for about 2 minutes.
   - **Add Lemon and Capers:** Stir in the lemon juice and capers. Let the sauce simmer for another 2 minutes, or until slightly reduced. If you prefer a richer sauce, whisk in the remaining tablespoon of butter until melted and smooth.
4. **Combine and Serve:**
   - **Return Chicken to Pan:** Return the cooked chicken breasts to the skillet, spooning the sauce over the top. Simmer for another minute or two to heat the chicken through.
   - **Garnish:** Garnish with chopped parsley and lemon slices if desired.

5. **Serve:**
    - **Enjoy:** Serve the Chicken Piccata over pasta, rice, or alongside roasted vegetables. Spoon extra sauce over the chicken for added flavor.

Tips

- **For Extra Flavor:** You can add a pinch of red pepper flakes to the sauce for a bit of heat.
- **Thickening the Sauce:** If you prefer a thicker sauce, you can mix 1 tablespoon of cornstarch with 1 tablespoon of water and stir it into the sauce during the last few minutes of cooking.

Enjoy your Chicken Piccata! It's a flavorful, elegant dish that's sure to impress.

Spicy Pork Ribs

Ingredients

For the Ribs:

- 2 racks of pork ribs (about 2-3 lbs each)
- 2 tbsp olive oil

For the Spice Rub:

- 2 tbsp smoked paprika
- 1 tbsp brown sugar
- 1 tbsp chili powder
- 1 tsp cayenne pepper (adjust to taste)
- 1 tsp garlic powder
- 1 tsp onion powder
- 1 tsp ground cumin
- 1 tsp dried oregano
- 1/2 tsp salt
- 1/2 tsp black pepper

For the Barbecue Sauce:

- 1 cup barbecue sauce (store-bought or homemade)
- 2 tbsp hot sauce (adjust to taste)
- 1 tbsp honey (optional, for added sweetness)
- 1 tbsp apple cider vinegar

Instructions

1. **Prepare the Ribs:**
   - **Remove the Membrane:** Place the ribs on a cutting board. Use a knife to gently lift and remove the thin membrane from the back of the ribs. This step helps make the ribs more tender.
   - **Season the Ribs:** Rub the ribs with olive oil. Generously coat both sides of the ribs with the spice rub, pressing it in to adhere.
2. **Cook the Ribs:**

   Oven Method:
   - **Preheat Oven:** Preheat your oven to 300°F (150°C).
   - **Prepare Ribs:** Place the ribs on a large piece of aluminum foil, bone-side down. Wrap the foil around the ribs to create a sealed packet.
   - **Bake:** Place the wrapped ribs on a baking sheet and bake in the preheated oven for 2.5 to 3 hours, or until the ribs are tender.
   - **Finish on Grill or Broiler (Optional):** For a crispy finish, preheat a grill or broiler. Unwrap the ribs from the foil and brush with the barbecue sauce mixture. Grill or broil for 5-10 minutes, turning and basting with additional sauce, until caramelized and slightly crispy.
3. **Grill Method:**
   - **Preheat Grill:** Preheat your grill to medium heat (about 350°F or 175°C).

- **Grill Ribs:** Place the ribs on the grill and cook over indirect heat for about 2-2.5 hours, with the grill lid closed. Turn occasionally and brush with barbecue sauce mixture during the last 30 minutes of cooking.
- **Finish with Sauce:** For a caramelized finish, move the ribs over direct heat and grill for a few minutes per side, brushing with more barbecue sauce and turning frequently.

4. **Prepare the Barbecue Sauce:**
   - **Combine Ingredients:** In a small bowl, mix together barbecue sauce, hot sauce, honey (if using), and apple cider vinegar. Adjust seasoning to taste.
5. **Serve:**
   - **Slice Ribs:** Once the ribs are cooked and tender, remove them from the heat and let them rest for a few minutes before slicing between the bones.
   - **Serve:** Serve the ribs with extra barbecue sauce on the side for dipping or drizzling.

Tips

- **For Extra Tender Ribs:** If you have time, marinate the ribs with the spice rub overnight in the refrigerator.
- **Adjust Spiciness:** Modify the amount of cayenne pepper and hot sauce in the rub and sauce to suit your preferred spice level.

Enjoy your Spicy Pork Ribs! They're perfect for a summer barbecue or a flavorful meal any time of year.